973.174   Hopkins, Lee   5542
Hop   Bennett

Important dates
in
Afro-American
history

DATE		
NOV 9		
SHS		
Fac 98-99		

5542

Important Dates in Afro-American History

IMPORTANT DATES IN AFRO-AMERICAN HISTORY

by
LEE BENNETT HOPKINS

Illustrated with photographs

Franklin Watts, Inc.
845 Third Avenue
New York, N.Y. 10022

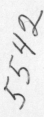

In memory of Dr. Martin Luther King, Jr.,
who lived so that black and white could share
a dream together—

and for Kimberly and Donald,
whose generation may see this dream through.

L.B.H.

ACKNOWLEDGMENTS

The quotations in this book are used by permission and special arrangements
with the proprietors of their respective copyrights who are listed below. Franklin Watts, Inc., has obtained permission for reprinting in this edition only. Any
requests for use of this material in any form must be directed to the copyright
holders who are listed herein.

Dodd, Mead & Company, Inc., for "The End of the Chapter" and "October"
from *The Complete Poems of Paul Laurence Dunbar*. Reprinted by permission of Dodd, Mead & Company, Inc.

Alfred A. Knopf, Inc., for the selection from "The Negro Speaks of Rivers," by
Langston Hughes. Copyright 1926 by Alfred A. Knopf, Inc., and renewed
1954 by Langston Hughes. Reprinted from *Selected Poems*, by Langston
Hughes, by permission of the publisher.

JANUARY

African Proverb

The coming year is not yet out of
sight. Let us be up and doing.

JANUARY 1

New Year's Day

Many people ring out the old year and ring in the new by making resolutions to change in the year ahead.

January 1, 1863, was a day on which the United States government announced its resolution to make a very important change. The Civil War was being fought. One of the issues that had led to the war was slavery in America. On this day President Abraham Lincoln issued the Emancipation Proclamation—a document that freed slaves in all territories at war with the Union. It was not until the end of the Civil War that the slaves were actually able to achieve the emancipation that Lincoln's document promised them.

President Abraham Lincoln wrote the first draft of the Emancipation Proclamation at a desk in the War Department telegraph office. NEW YORK PUBLIC LIBRARY, PICTURE COLLECTION

JANUARY 3

NEWS NOTE—1966

Robert C. Henry takes office as mayor of Springfield, Ohio.

Henry's victory at the polls in November, 1965, made him the first black mayor in the state of Ohio.

JANUARY 5

Death of George Washington Carver (1864–1943)

Look at a peanut. How important do you think it is? What can you do with it? Most people would think of eating it or making peanut butter. Dr. George Washington Carver, one of America's leading scientists, experimented with the

Scientist George Washington Carver (wearing suit) at work in a laboratory at Tuskegee Institute. CULVER PICTURES, INC.

peanut, and found more than three hundred products that could be made from it, including wood dyes, soap, linoleum, plastics, flour, paint, ink, and many different kinds of oil.

Dr. Carver worked to improve the economy of the South through his experiments, not only with the peanut, but with sweet potatoes, soybeans, and cotton stalks, as well.

In the state of New York, January 5 is known as Carver Day.

Many of Dr. Carver's personal belongings and scientific papers are housed in the Carver Museum on the campus of Tuskegee Institute in Alabama, where he served as director of agricultural research.

JANUARY 7

NEWS NOTE—1955

Marian Anderson becomes the first black singer to perform with the Metropolitan Opera. She makes this debut in Verdi's *A Masked Ball*, and *The New York Times* reports the event on its front page.

Marian Anderson takes a curtain call at the Metropolitan Opera following her performance in Verdi's *A Masked Ball*. HUROK ATTRACTIONS

JANUARY 9

NEWS NOTE—1866

Fisk University opens in Nashville, Tennessee, as an elementary school, beginning with the first grade.

Later Fisk begins to train teachers and administrators. Today the university is a great center for blacks seeking higher education.

Jubilee Hall, a women's residence at Fisk University, built with funds raised by the Fisk Jubilee Singers. PHOTO BY JOHN SWEITZER, FISK UNIVERSITY

JANUARY 12

Birthday of James Farmer (1920–   )

James Farmer was one of the founders of the Congress of Racial Equality (CORE), an organization originally

In July, 1965, James Farmer, then National Director of CORE, arrives in Bogalusa, Louisiana, to lead a civil rights march. UNITED PRESS INTERNATIONAL

dedicated to nonviolent direct action to end social and economic discrimination. CORE was particularly active in the 1961 Freedom Rides that tested the desegregation of public waiting rooms and restaurants of interstate bus companies in the South. Farmer served as national director of the organization until 1966.

In 1968, Farmer, running on both the Republican and Liberal tickets, lost the election to the United States Congress from the twelfth district in Brooklyn, New York. That same year he was active in the Black Independents and

7

Democrats, a group that supported Nelson A. Rockefeller in his unsuccessful attempt to win the 1968 Republican nomination for President.

In 1969, Farmer was named an Assistant Secretary of Health, Education and Welfare under the Administration of President Richard Nixon. He resigned from that post in December, 1970.

Farmer was born in Marshall, Texas.

JANUARY 13

NEWS NOTE—1966

Dr. Robert C. Weaver is appointed Secretary of the newly established Department of Housing and Urban Development by President Lyndon B. Johnson, making him the first black American to serve in the Cabinet of a United States President.

Weaver was born on December 29, 1907, in Washington, D.C.

JANUARY 15

Birthday of Martin Luther King, Jr. (1929–1968)

Martin Luther King, Jr., adopted his name from the great Protestant Reformation minister Martin Luther; King was born Michael Lewis King.

After graduating from Morehouse College in 1948, King

The Reverend Martin Luther King, Jr., speaking at the 1963 March on Washington. PICTORIAL PARADE.

decided to enter the ministry. He received a Bachelor of Divinity degree from Crozier Theological Seminary in Chester, Pennsylvania. Continuing his education, he received a Doctor of Philosophy degree in 1955 from Boston University.

Dr. King received many awards for his nonviolent direct-action approach in seeking to establish the civil rights of all Americans. In leading the campaign for immediate equality for his people he counseled against engaging in acts of a violent nature, even when attacked. In 1963, *Time* magazine chose him Man of the Year because of his protests against segregation in Birmingham, Alabama. In 1964, he became the second black American to receive the Nobel Peace Prize, an international award granted to the person judged to have made the greatest contribution to the promotion of international peace within a given year.

On August 28, 1963, Dr. King addressed more than 200,000 Americans who congregated at a march on Washington, D.C., to protest against racial inequality in the United States. The following lines are from the moving speech he delivered at the march:

I have a dream today.

I have a dream that one day every valley shall be exalted. . . .

This will be the day when all of God's children will be able to sing with new meaning:

"My country 'tis of thee,
Sweet land of liberty,
Of thee I sing:
Land where my fathers died,
Land of the Pilgrims' pride,
From every mountain-side
Let Freedom ring."

And if America is to be a great nation, this must come true. So let freedom ring from the prodigious hilltops of New Hampshire. Let freedom ring from the mighty mountains of New York. Let freedom ring from the heightening Alleghenies of Pennsylvania. Let freedom ring from the snow-capped Rockies of Colorado. Let freedom ring from the curvacious slopes of California. But not only that, let freedom ring from Stone Mountain of Georgia.

Let freedom ring from Lookout Mountain of Tennessee.

Let freedom ring from every hill and molehill of Mississippi. From every mountainside, let freedom ring. And when we allow freedom to ring, when we let it ring from every village, from every hamlet, from every state and every city, we will be able to speed up that day when all of God's children, black men and white men, Jews and Gentiles, Protestants and Catholics, will be able to join hands and sing in the words of the old Negro spiritual: "Free at last! Free at last! Thank God almighty, we are free at last!"

On April 4, 1968, Martin Luther King, Jr., was shot to death in Memphis, Tennessee, while fighting for the rights of that city's sanitation workers.

He was buried in Atlanta, Georgia, the place of his birth, on April 9, 1968.

11

Birthday of Paul Cuffe (1759–1817)

Paul Cuffe (also spelled "Cuffee") had a love for the sea and became a sailor while still in his teens. Later, he turned his energies to shipbuilding and established a successful business.

Cuffe wanted to improve the living conditions of all black

A monument to Captain Paul Cuffe stands on the Friends Meeting House property in Central Village, Westport, Massachusetts. PHOTO BY EUGENE LONGFIELD, PRESIDENT, WESTPORT CHAMBER OF COMMERCE

Americans. In New Bedford, Massachusetts, where he was born, black children had no schools of their own and were not allowed to go to school with whites. To provide his own children with an education, Cuffe built a school, hired a teacher, and opened the doors to all the black youngsters in New Bedford.

In the early 1800's, he led the first movement to resettle

black Americans in Africa. He succeeded in establishing a special colony called the Friendship Society, in Sierra Leone, a small British colony on the western coast of Africa. The movement ended when Cuffe died on September 9, 1817.

In 1913, Cuffe's great-grandson, Horatio Howard, erected a five-foot monument to the memory of Paul Cuffe, in Westport, Massachusetts, a small village near Cuffe's birthplace.

JANUARY 18

Birthday of Daniel Hale Williams (1856–1931)

When Daniel Hale Williams was thirty-five years old, President Grover Cleveland named him Surgeon General of Freedmen's Hospital in Washington, D.C.

After serving in this government hospital for five years, he went on to the Cook County Hospital in Chicago, and then to St. Luke's Hospital, also in Chicago.

On July 10, 1893, at Provident Hospital in Chicago, Dr. Williams performed the first successful heart operation on record.

Williams was born in Holidaysburg, Pennsylvania.

Dr. Daniel Hale Williams, surgeon and founder of Provident Hospital in Chicago, where he performed the first successful heart surgery on record. NEW YORK PUBLIC LIBRARY, SCHOMBURG COLLECTION

Editor and publisher John H. Johnson owns the Johnson Publishing Co., Inc., and publishes *The Negro Digest, Ebony, Tan,* and *Jet.* COURTESY OF THE JOHNSON PUBLISHING CO., INC.

JANUARY 19

Birthday of John H. Johnson (1918–   )

John H. Johnson is one of the busiest men in American publishing. The company he owns publishes four major magazines—*The Negro Digest, Ebony, Tan,* and *Jet.*

Johnson was born in Arkansas City, Arkansas. As a teenager he attended Du Sable High School, in Chicago, where he was editor of his school paper and class yearbook. You can find his magazines on newsstands and in libraries throughout the United States.

JANUARY 25

NEWS NOTE—1966

Constance Baker Motley becomes the first black woman to be appointed a federal judge.

JANUARY 27

NEWS NOTE—1872

Charlotte E. Ray becomes the first known black woman lawyer in the United States. She was graduated from Howard University Law School, in Washington, D.C.

JANUARY 29

NEWS NOTE—1969

Shirley Chisholm, first black congresswoman in the United States, is successful in her fight against appointment to the House Agriculture Committee. Mrs. Chisholm bases her plea on the fact that the subcommittee on Forestry and Rural Villages to which she was assigned is meaningless

First black congress-woman, Shirley Chisholm, with then President Lyndon B. Johnson. UNITED PRESS INTERNATIONAL

to the people in the predominantly black and Puerto Rican Bedford-Stuyvesant area of Brooklyn, New York, which she represents. Mrs. Chisholm is the first member of Congress to fight such a committee appointment.

JANUARY 29

NEWS NOTE—1969

Patricia Roberts Harris is named dean of Howard University's law school. In 1965, President Lyndon B. Johnson appointed Mrs. Harris United States Ambassador to Luxembourg, making her the first black woman to hold such a post.

JANUARY 31

NEWS NOTE—1962

Lieutenant Commander Samuel L. Gravely becomes the first black commander of a United States warship, as he takes command of the destroyer escort U.S.S. Falgout.

Did You Know That

Georg Olden was the first black American to design a United States postage stamp? The stamp was issued in 1963, to commemorate the hundredth anniversary of the Emancipation Proclamation.

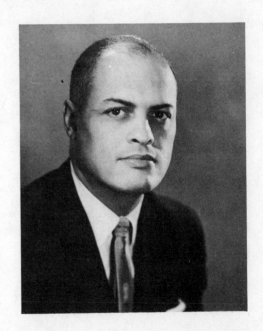

Georg Olden, first black American to design a United States postage stamp. COURTESY OF THE OFFICE OF THE POSTMASTER GENERAL

FEBRUARY

African Proverb

Better lose all money than all friendship.

FEBRUARY 1

NEWS NOTE—1865

John H. Rock becomes the first black lawyer admitted to practice before the United States Supreme Court.

FEBRUARY 1

Birthday of Langston Hughes (1902–1967)

Langston Hughes is one of the best-loved poets in America. He was born in Joplin, Missouri, and attended high school in Cleveland, Ohio. In 1929, he graduated from Lincoln University, in Pennsylvania, and went to New

Author Langston Hughes. PHOTO BY ROY DE CARAVA

York City. Many of Hughes's poems were written about America's blacks—his people. One of his most famous is "The Negro Speaks of Rivers," which he wrote on the back of an envelope while on a train ride to Mexico. In this poem he wrote:

. . . My soul has grown deep like the rivers.

I bathed in the Euphrates when dawns were young,
I built my hut near the Congo and it lulled me to sleep.
I looked upon the Nile and raised the pyramids above it . . .

My soul has grown deep like the rivers.

In addition to poetry, Hughes wrote novels, children's books, short stories, operas, plays and operettas, and newspaper columns. It was in a newspaper that he created the character Jesse B. Semple, who became a familiar figure (known as Simple) to millions of Americans. Simple's problems were typical of those faced by black men. Langston Hughes died in his beloved Harlem in New York City on May 22, 1967.

FEBRUARY 9

Death of Paul Laurence Dunbar (1872–1906)

Paul Laurence Dunbar is one of America's best-known black poets. His early poetry, written in dialect, earned him a national reputation. *The Complete Poems*, a volume of Dunbar's poems published in 1913, has never been out

Poet Paul Laurence Dunbar. BROWN
BROTHERS

of print. It includes both humor and dialect and sensitive
and touching verse. You can find lines from his poem
"October" on page 151, and from his "End of the Chapter"
on page 184. Dunbar died of pneumonia at the age of thirty-
four.

FEBRUARY 10

Birthday of Leontyne Price (1927–   )

Leontyne Price is one of the world's great lyric sopranos.
Born in Laurel, Mississippi, she earned a Bachelor of Sci-
ence degree from Central State College, in Wilberforce,
Ohio.

World-renowned lyric soprano Leontyne Price. PHOTO BY HUBERT DILWORTH

On January 27, 1961, she made her debut with the Metropolitan Opera in New York, in Verdi's *Il Trovatore*. She was immediately acclaimed Musician of the Year by a group of editors and music critics.

In September, 1966, when the new Metropolitan Opera House opened in New York, Miss Price sang the lead in the debut of *Antony and Cleopatra*, an opera written for her by Samuel Barber.

FEBRUARY 12

Birthday of Abraham Lincoln (1809–1865)

The sixteenth President of the United States, Abraham Lincoln, came from a simple background. He was born on the American frontier in Hardin County, Kentucky. He became a lawyer through self-education and served in the House of Representatives from 1847 to 1849. In 1856, he joined the newly formed Republican party to fight against the extension of slavery to new states and territories.

Lincoln became a national figure in 1858, when he won the race for senator from Illinois against Senator Stephen A. Douglas, a proslavery Democrat. Not long after his election as President in 1860, Lincoln was faced with a split nation—seven Southern states seceded from the Union. From that point on, his main purpose was to preserve the Union; he attempted to win the South's return without war —even modifying his own position on slavery. It was only

This statue of Abraham Lincoln stands on the steps of the High Street Courthouse in Newark, New Jersey. UNITED PRESS INTERNATIONAL

after a year and a half of Civil War that he issued his famous Emancipation Proclamation, which freed the slaves in areas rebelling against the Union.

Lincoln was assassinated on April 15, 1865. In many parts of the United States you can find a shrine, a piece of sculpture, a statue, a monument, or a street named after him. Some of the places which honor his name are:

Lincoln Center for the Performing Arts, New York.
Lincoln Highway, stretching from New York to San Francisco.
Lincoln Memorial, Washington, D.C.

The face of Abraham Lincoln is carved in stone at Mount Rushmore in South Dakota, and the capital of Nebraska is named Lincoln.

What places do you know that bear Lincoln's name?

FEBRUARY 12–20

NEWS NOTE

The week that includes both the date of Abraham Lincoln's birth and Frederick Douglass' death is celebrated as Negro History Week. It was started in 1926 by Carter G. Woodson, a black historian.

FEBRUARY 14

NEWS NOTE—1867

Augusta Institute opens in Atlanta, Georgia. Later it becomes Morehouse College, the school attended by the Reverend Martin Luther King, Jr.

Public funeral services for Dr. King were conducted at Morehouse on April 9, 1968.

FEBRUARY 14

Birthday of Moneta Sleet, Jr. (1926–   )

Moneta Sleet, Jr., was the winner of the 1969 Pulitzer Prize in photography. He received the award for a photograph of Mrs. Martin Luther King, Jr., and her daughter Bernice, taken at the funeral services for Dr. King in Atlanta on April 9, 1968. The photograph, widely used in newspapers and magazines, captures the grief and the courage of Mrs. King.

Sleet was born in Owensboro, Kentucky. He graduated from Kentucky State College and the School of Modern Photography in New York City, and received his Master's degree in journalism from New York University. After World War II, he became an instructor of photography at Maryland State College. From 1950 to 1955 Sleet was on assignment for *Our World* magazine. Since 1955 he has worked for *Ebony* magazine. He lives in Baldwin, Long Island, in New York State.

The Southern Christian Leadership Conference (SCLC) was organized on this date, with Dr. Martin Luther King, Jr., as its president. Its headquarters are in Atlanta, Georgia. One of SCLC's aims is to provide "full citizenship rights and total integration of the Negro into American life." SCLC seeks to end segregation through such nonviolent direct action as economic boycotts, protest demonstrations, marches, and sit-ins. Advocates of nonviolent direct action believe that one should never resort to violence, even when confronted by violent opponents. They seek change by calling public attention to what they feel are social, political, and economic injustices.

The Reverend Ralph Abernathy became president of SCLC in 1968, after the assassination of Dr. King.

FEBRUARY 15

NEWS NOTE—1915

The first Spingarn Medal, an annual award presented by the National Association for the Advancement of Colored People (NAACP), is given to Ernest E. Just. Just was a biologist who had conducted research on fertilization and cell division.

Biologist Ernest E. Just, winner of the first Spingarn Medal in 1915. THE ASSOCIATED PUBLISHERS

FEBRUARY 17

Birthday of Jim Brown (1936–   )

Today, Jim Brown is known to Americans as a popular film star. In 1966, he announced his retirement from the world of sports to begin a movie career.

Brown was born on St. Simon Island in Georgia, but spent most of his childhood years in Manhasset, Long Island, in New York. While attending Manhasset High School, his extraordinary talents in sports were recognized. At graduation he had forty-two college scholarships offered him and two professional offers—from the New York Yankees and the Boston Braves. Brown accepted the scholarship from Syracuse University where he became an All-American star in football and lacrosse. In 1957, he played with the Cleveland Browns and was named Rookie of the Year.

His record until his retirement was a fantastic one, making him the greatest running back professional football has ever known.

FEBRUARY 20

Death of Frederick Augustus Douglass (1817–1895)

Frederick Augustus Washington Bailey, born a slave in Tuckahoe, Talbot County, Maryland, was a journalist, statesman, and an important figure in the movement to abolish slavery. At the age of twenty-one, he escaped from his master, changed his name to Douglass, and made his way to New Bed-

Frederick Douglass was a writer, editor, and abolitionist. NEW YORK PUBLIC LIBRARY, SCHOMBURG COLLECTION

ford, Massachusetts, by way of Baltimore and New York. Shortly afterward, Douglass lectured before antislavery societies in Massachusetts, Great Britain, and Ireland. He returned to the United States, bought his freedom, and remained active as editor of *The North Star*, an antislavery newspaper.

At the beginning of the Civil War, Douglass urged President Lincoln to recruit black soldiers. The first two black men to join the Northern army were Douglass' own sons.

There are many memorials honoring Douglass: At 1411 West Street, N.E., in Washington, D.C., you can visit the home in which he spent the last thirteen years of his life; a statue of him stands in a public park in Rochester, New York; and in New York City, a street in Harlem bears the name Frederick Douglass Circle.

FEBRUARY 20

Birthday of Sidney Poitier (1924–   )

Sidney Poitier is one of Hollywood's leading film stars. He made history on April 14, 1964, when he became the first black man to win an Academy Award Oscar for best actor (of 1963). Poitier received the Oscar—the highest honor given by the Motion Picture Academy—for his role in the film *Lilies of the Field*.

FEBRUARY 22

NEWS NOTE—1950

Dr. Ralph J. Bunche is awarded the Nobel Peace Prize for his success as United Nations mediator in working out a truce between Egypt and Israel, following the 1948 war in the Middle East. Dr. Bunche is the first black American to receive this coveted award.

Nobel Peace Prize-winner Dr. Ralph Bunche, United Nations Undersecretary for Special Political Affairs, visits with one of his elementary-school teachers. UNITED PRESS INTERNATIONAL

FEBRUARY 23

Birthday of William Edward Burghardt DuBois (1868–1963)

W.E.B. DuBois was a scientist, scholar, historian, writer, poet, teacher, and editor. He was born in Great Barrington, Massachusetts, and died at the age of ninety-five, on the eve of the 1963 civil rights march on Washington. At the time of his death DuBois was a citizen of Ghana, where

W.E.B. DuBois, who urged blacks to develop themselves culturally and intellectually, was an important leader of the twentieth century. BROWN BROTHERS

he went by invitation of the government in 1961. He lived in Accra and worked there editing the *Encyclopedia Africana*.

Hiram R. Revels, the first black United States senator.
LIBRARY OF CONGRESS

FEBRUARY 25

NEWS NOTE—1870

Hiram R. Revels takes the oath of office in the United States Senate, to become the first black senator.

Revels represented the state of Mississippi until March 3, 1871.

FEBRUARY 27

Birthday of Marian Anderson (1902–   )

The singing career of Marian Anderson was launched at the age of seventeen, when she was the winner in a contest among three hundred singers at Lewisohn Stadium in New York City. Miss Anderson again sang at Lewisohn Stadium with the New York Philharmonic on August 26, 1925.

Marian Anderson is famous for her rich contralto voice. COURTESY OF HURQK AT-TRACTIONS

She was refused permission to perform in many states because she was black. A scheduled concert at Constitution Hall in Washington, D.C., was canceled by the Daughters of the American Revolution, who owned the premises. Mrs. Franklin Delano Roosevelt, the wife of the United States President, contested this discrimination, and Marian Anderson received a special invitation to sing on Easter Sunday, 1939, at the Lincoln Memorial. Thousands of people gathered to hear her sing Negro spirituals and to hear her voice echo the words to "America."

During this same year the National Association for the Advancement of Colored People (NAACP) awarded her the Spingarn Medal in recognition of her special achievement in the field of music. The medal was presented to her by Mrs. Roosevelt in Richmond, Virginia, at the NAACP's thirtieth annual conference.

When the famous conductor Arturo Toscanini heard the

Philadelphia-born singer perform, he said, "She has a voice that is heard only once in one hundred years." Miss Anderson's rich contralto voice has been heard at the Metropolitan Opera House in New York and in cities throughout the United States.

Each year the Spingarn Medal is awarded to a black American who has made the greatest contribution in his field? The medal was established by Joel Elias Spingarn (1875–1939), an American publisher, literary critic, and chairman of the board of directors of the National Association for the Advancement of Colored People.

The first medal was awarded to Professor Ernest E. Just in 1915 for his research in biology. Medal winners of the 1960's include:

1960—Langston Hughes, for literature.

1961—Kenneth B. Clark, for research in psychology and for the organization of a child-development center.

1962—Robert C. Weaver, for developing a doctrine of "open occupancy" in housing.

1963—Medgar Wiley Evers, for dedication to the fight for freedom.

1964—Roy Wilkins, for contributing to the advancement of the American people and to the national purpose.

1965—Leontyne Price, for outstanding achievements in the field of opera.

1966—John H. Johnson, for preeminence in Negro publishing.

1967—Edward W. Brooke III, for his distinguished career as a public servant.

1968—Sammy Davis, Jr., for his many achievements in the field of entertainment and in the civil rights movement.

1969—Clarence M. Mitchell, Jr., for his political achievement.

1970—Jacob Lawrence, for achievement in art forms.

MARCH

MARCH 1

Birthday of Blanche Kelso Bruce (1841–1898)

Blanche K. Bruce was born a slave in Prince Edward County, Virginia, but escaped to the North. He attended Oberlin College, in Ohio. After the Civil War, he returned to the South and settled in Mississippi.

On March 5, 1875, he took the oath of office as United States senator from Mississippi, thus becoming the second black United States senator—the first to serve a full term (1875–81).

MARCH 1

Birthday of Harry Belafonte, Jr. (1927–   )

Before launching his theatrical career, Harry Belafonte worked as a janitor. He was born in New York City, but

Folk singer Harry Belafonte.
UNITED PRESS INTERNATIONAL

moved to the West Indies at the age of eight. At thirteen, he returned to New York, where he attended high school before joining the Navy. His musical career flourished in the 1950's, and his recordings of folk music were heard throughout the world. He studied folk music by reading a great deal of folklore, by poring over folk archives in the United States Library of Congress, and by talking to sailors, field hands, road workers, farmers—the people who created the songs he sings.

MARCH 3

NEWS NOTE—1886

R. F. Flemming, Jr., a black inventor, is granted a patent for a guitar.

MARCH 5

Death of Crispus Attucks (1723?–1770)

On the night of March 5, 1770, Crispus Attucks, a former slave, along with four white men, Samuel Gray, James Caldwell, Patrick Carr, and Samuel Maverick, was shot down by British soldiers in what is known as the Boston Massacre. The men were part of a crowd gathered in front of the Custom House. Friction between Boston's citizens and the British soldiers had been building up. March 5 was

The 29th Regiment have already left us, and the 14th Regiment are following them, so that we expect the Town will soon be clear of all the Troops. The Wisdom and true Policy of his Majesty's Council and Col. Dalrymple the Commander appear in this Measure. Two Regiments in the midst of this populous City, and the Inhabitants justly incensed: Those of the neighbouring Towns actually under Arms upon the first Report of the Massacre, and the Signal only wanting to bring in a few Hours to the Gates of this City many Thousands of our brave Brethren in the Country, deeply affected with our Distresses, and to whom we are greatly obliged on this Occasion—No one knows where this would have ended, and what important Consequences even to the whole British Empire might have followed, which our Moderation and Loyalty upon so trying an Occasion, and our Faith in the Commander's Assurances have happily prevented.

Last Thursday, agreeable to a general Request of the Inhabitants, and by the Consent of Parents and Friends, were carried to their Grave in Succession, the Bodies of *Samuel Gray*, *Samuel Maverick*, *James Caldwell*, and *Crispus Attucks*, the unhappy Victims who fell in the bloody Massacre of the day Evening preceding!

On this Occasion most of the Shops in Town were shut, all the Bells were ordered to toll a solemn Peal, as were also those in the neighboring Towns of Charlestown Roxbury, &c. The Procession began to move between the Hours of 4 and 5 in the Afternoon; two of the unfortunate Sufferers, viz. Mess. *James Caldwell* and *Crispus Attucks*, who were Strangers, borne from Faneuil-Hall, attended by a numerous Train of Persons of all Ranks; and the other two, viz. Mr. *Samuel Gray*, from the House of Mr. Benjamin Gray, (his Brother) on the North-side the Exchange, and Mr. *Maverick*, from the House of his distressed Mother Mrs. *Mary Maverick*, in Union-Street, each followed by their respective Relations and Friends: The several Hearses forming a Junction in King-Street, the Theatre of that inhuman Tragedy! proceeded from thence thro' the Main-Street, lengthened by an immense Concourse of People, so numerous as to be obliged to follow in Ranks of six, and brought up by a long Train of Carriages belonging to the principal Gentry of the Town. The Bodies were deposited in one Vault in the middle Burying-ground: The aggravated Circumstances of their Death, the Distress and Sorrow visible in every Countenance, together with the peculiar Solemnity with which the whole Funeral was conducted, surpass Description.

The initials of Crispus Attucks mark the coffin on the far right in an account of the Boston Massacre in the Boston *Gazette and Country Journal*. NEW YORK PUBLIC LIBRARY, SCHOMBURG COLLECTION

the night when the trouble finally erupted and the soldiers fired on the Bostonians.

A monument stands on the Boston Common, in Boston, Massachusetts, to honor these men—the first martyrs to the cause of American independence. In the upper right-hand corner of this monument, an inscription by John Adams reads:

On that night the foundation of American Independence was laid.

MARCH 5

NEWS NOTE—1875

Blanche Kelso Bruce of Mississippi takes his seat in the United States Senate.

He becomes the first black senator to fill a complete term (1875–81).

MARCH 6

NEWS NOTE—1957

Ghana, one of Africa's smallest lands, receives independence from Great Britain and is the first black African colony to become an independent nation. Upon independence Kwame Nkrumah became Ghana's first president.

Kwame Nkrumah, first president of Ghana, the first black African colony to become independent, addresses the United Nations General Assembly. UNITED NATIONS

African nations to receive their independence after Ghana are:

Nation:	Date:
Algeria	July 3, 1962
Botswana	September 30, 1966
Burundi	July 1, 1962
Cameroon	January 1, 1960
Central African Republic	August 13, 1960
Chad	August 11, 1960
Congo (Brazzaville)	August 15, 1960
Congo (Kinshasa)	June 30, 1960
Dahomey	August 1, 1960
Equatorial Guinea	October 12, 1968
Gabon	August 17, 1960
Gambia, The	February 18, 1965
Guinea	October 2, 1958
Ivory Coast	August 7, 1960
Kenya	December 12, 1963
Lesotho	October 4, 1966
Malagasy Republic	June 26, 1960
Malawi	July 6, 1964
Mali	June 20, 1960
Mauritania	November 28, 1960
Niger	August 3, 1960
Nigeria	October 1, 1960
Rwanda	July 1, 1962
Senegal	June 20, 1960
Sierra Leone	April 27, 1961
Somalia	July 1, 1960
Swaziland	September 6, 1968

Tanzania*

Tanganyika and	December 9, 1961
Zanzibar	December 10, 1963
Togo	April 27, 1960
Uganda	October 9, 1962
Upper Volta	August 5, 1960
Zambia	October 24, 1964

In addition to the above list, Rhodesia declared itself independent from the United Kingdom on November 11, 1965; and on May 30, 1967, what was the Eastern Region of Nigeria declared its independence as the Republic of Biafra. However, at the time of this printing the overwhelming majority of the world's nations recognize neither Rhodesia nor Biafra.

MARCH 9

Birthday of Oscar De Priest (1871–1951)

In 1929, Oscar De Priest entered the United States House of Representatives as congressman from Illinois.

* In October, 1964, Tanganyika and Zanzibar united to form the nation of Tanzania.

Oscar De Priest of Illinois was the first black congressman in the twentieth century. LIBRARY OF CONGRESS

He was the first black American elected to Congress in the twentieth century.

De Priest, who was born in Florence, Alabama, spent most of his life in politics.

MARCH 10

Death of Harriet Tubman (1821?–1913)

Harriet Tubman was born in Dorchester County, Maryland, in slavery.

The tablet which was placed near her home in Auburn, New York, a year after her death, beautifully and simply tells the story of her life.

> In memory of Harriet Tubman.
> Born a slave in Maryland about 1821.

Harriet Tubman was called the "Moses of her people" because she led so many slaves to freedom via the Underground Railroad. NEW YORK PUBLIC LIBRARY, SCHOMBURG COLLECTION

Died in Auburn, N.Y., March 10th, 1913.
Called the Moses of her people,
During the Civil War. With rare
Courage she led over three hundred
Negroes up from slavery to freedom,
And rendered invaluable service
As nurse and spy.
With implicit trust in God
She braved every danger and
Overcame every obstacle. Withal
She possessed extraordinary
Foresight and judgment so that
She truthfully said
"On my Underground Railroad
I nebber run my train off de track
An' I nebber los' a passenger."
This tablet is erected
By the citizens of Auburn.

Birthday of Ralph David Abernathy (1926–   )

Associated with Dr. Martin Luther King, Jr., in all phases of the nonviolent civil rights movement, Dr. Ralph Abernathy became the head of the Southern Christian Leadership Conference (SCLC) upon the assassination of Dr. King in 1968.

Abernathy was born the tenth of twelve children in Linden, Alabama, a small town in the heart of the Black Belt, where his parents owned about five hundred acres of farmland.

At the age of seventeen Abernathy felt the call to devote

The Reverend Ralph Abernathy helps put up a shack for "Resurrection City, U.S.A." as part of the 1968 Poor People's Campaign in Washington, D.C. The campaign sought to bring public attention to the plight of poor Americans. UNITED PRESS INTERNATIONAL

his life to God. In 1948, at twenty-two, he was ordained a Baptist minister. He received his Bachelor of Science degree from Alabama College two years later; his Master of Arts degree in sociology from Atlanta University in 1957; and an LL.D. degree from Allen University, in Columbia, South Carolina, in 1960.

After Dr. King's death Abernathy carried out the plan for a Poor People's March on Washington, D.C., in the spring of 1968. Resurrection City, a village of temporary shelters, was erected. Its inhabitants visited congressmen to press the campaign for the rights of poor people in America. Wide support was given to the campaign by many Americans. Among the famous entertainers who gave their services to the city were Sidney Poitier, Marlon Brando, Bill Cosby, and Barbra Streisand.

Dr. Abernathy and his family live in Atlanta, Georgia, where he continues to do the work he started with Dr. King and SCLC.

MARCH 11

NEWS NOTE—1959

Lorraine Hansberry's *A Raisin in the Sun* becomes the first play written by a black woman to appear on Broadway. The play is the first with a black director, Lloyd Richards, in over half a century.

With Sidney Poitier in the leading role, the play runs for over a year on Broadway, on an extensive cross-country tour, and is made into a motion picture.

Playwright Lorraine Hansberry wrote the successful play *A Raisin in the Sun*. UNITED PRESS INTERNATIONAL

MARCH 16

NEWS NOTE—1827

The first black newspaper in the United States, *Freedom's Journal,* begins publication in New York City. Its founders are Samuel E. Cornish and John Russwurm.

MARCH 18

Birthday of Norbert Rillieux (1806–1894)

Norbert Rillieux was an important scientist who invented a modern method of refining sugar. His methods were adopted in Cuba, Mexico, and throughout Europe, as well as in the United States.

A memorial to Rillieux in the Louisiana State Museum in New Orleans bears the inscription:

To honor and commemorate
Norbert Rillieux
Born at New Orleans, Louisiana, March 18, 1806,
and died at Paris, France, October 8, 1894.
Inventor of Multiple Evaporation and its
Application into the Sugar Industry.

MARCH 20

NEWS NOTE—1883

Patent No. 274,207 is granted to Jan Ernst Matzeliger (1852–89) for his invention of the lasting machine.

This device makes possible the manufacture of shoes by machine.

MARCH 30

NEWS NOTE—1870

The Fifteenth Amendment becomes part of the United States Constitution. It forbids any state to deny the right to vote because of "race, color, or previous condition of servitude."

Did You Know That

At the close of the Civil War, approximately 90 percent of America's black citizens were living in the South?

APRIL

African Proverb

The butterfly that brushes against thorns will tear
its wings.

APRIL 1–24

NEWS NOTE—1966

The first World Festival of Negro Arts is held in Dakar, Senegal, in West Africa, under the joint sponsorship of the United Nations Educational, Scientific and Cultural Organization (UNESCO), the government of Senegal, and the Society for the Study of African Culture. The festival features the artistic and musical talents of black people from all over the world.

APRIL 4

NEWS NOTE—1968

The Reverend Martin Luther King, Jr., is assassinated in Memphis, Tennessee. Dr. King was in Memphis leading a march aimed at securing decent wages for the city's sanitation workers.

The United States observed a national mourning period of six days in memory of its great civil rights leader who believed in ending segregation and racial injustice through nonviolent direct action.

United States Congressman Robert Smalls of South Carolina. LIBRARY OF CONGRESS

APRIL 5

Birthday of Robert Smalls (1839–1916)

Beaufort, South Carolina, a town near the sea, was where Robert Smalls was born a slave. When the Civil War broke out, Smalls was twenty-three years old. His master allowed him to work as a stevedore on the Confederate naval ship *The Planter*—one of the fastest and most valuable ships in the Confederate navy.

Smalls noticed that the officers, all of whom were white, often would spend the night ashore. He devised a daring plan, which he shared with other crewmen: On an evening when the crew was left alone on the ship, they would lift anchor, sail for Charleston Harbor, and turn the vessel over to the Union navy.

May 13, 1862, was the day they chose to carry out the

plan. Smalls smuggled his family on board and *The Planter* sailed to freedom.

Smalls received high praise and a large reward for his heroic deed. The following year he was made captain of *The Planter* and placed in command for the rest of the war. After the war, he served in the South Carolina legislature and became a major general in the state militia. From 1875 to 1886, he served three terms in the United States House of Representatives. White Southern racists managed to have him jailed for "corruption," but his supporters reelected him to the House. Smalls helped create the marine base at Parris Island, where thousands of Americans who served in the armed services were trained.

He died in 1916 at the age of seventy-six.

APRIL 5

Birthday of Booker Taliaferro Washington (1856–1915)

Booker T. Washington was the first black American elected to the Hall of Fame, at New York University, in New York City. On the base of the bust of Washington are the following lines from one of his speeches:

> The highest test of the civilization of a race is its willingness to extend a helping hand to the less fortunate.

Washington was founder of the Tuskegee Institute in Alabama—a school now famous throughout the world for agricultural research. The school was founded on his belief

Booker T. Washington in 1881, when he founded Tuskegee Institute. NEW YORK PUBLIC LIBRARY, SCHOMBURG COLLECTION

that the road to equality was through education. Washington died on November 14, 1915.

APRIL 6

Birthday of James Augustine Healy (1830–1900)

James Healy was born in Georgia to an Irish planter and a mulatto slave. Taken north in 1837, he was placed in

Bishop James Augustine Healy, the first black Roman Catholic bishop in the United States. NEW YORK PUBLIC LIBRARY, SCHOMBURG COLLECTION

a Quaker school in New York State. In 1849 he graduated from Holy Cross College. Five years later, at the Notre Dame Cathedral in Paris, he was ordained a priest. In 1875, Father Healy was named bishop of Portland, Maine— making him the first black Roman Catholic bishop in the United States.

APRIL 6

NEWS NOTE—1909

Matthew Henson, an explorer with Commander Robert E. Peary's expedition, places the United States flag on the North Pole. Henson is actually the first man to reach the Pole.

Matthew Henson, the first man to reach the North Pole, was in the party of famous explorer Robert Peary. NEW YORK PUBLIC LIBRARY, SCHOMBURG COLLECTION

APRIL 7

NEWS NOTE—1940

The Booker T. Washington stamp, the first United States postage stamp honoring a black person, goes on sale at Tuskegee Institute, before being distributed throughout the country.

APRIL 9

Birthday of Paul Robeson (1898–   )

Paul Robeson is known throughout the world for his acting and singing. His stage roles include *All God's Chillun Got Wings*, *The Hairy Ape*, and *Othello*. His Broad-

Paul Robeson (left) shakes hands with W.E.B. DuBois. UNITED PRESS INTERNATIONAL

way opening in 1943 as Othello received an ovation that was called "one of the most prolonged and wildest . . . in the history of the New York theater." Robeson's achievements in whatever he undertook were remarkable: he succeeded as an athlete, a scholar, an actor, and a singer.

APRIL 11

NEWS NOTE—1968

President Lyndon B. Johnson signs the Civil Rights Act of 1968. The Senate-approved civil rights bill, which passed

President Lyndon B. Johnson signs the 1968 Civil Rights Act. UNITED PRESS INTERNATIONAL

the House of Representatives on April 10 by a vote of 250 to 171, establishes open housing as law. According to the new law:

It is the policy of the United States to provide, within constitutional limitations, for fair housing throughout the United States.

Discrimination is banned in the sale of most housing "against any person . . . because of race, color, religion, or national origin."

APRIL 14

NEWS NOTE—1964

Sidney Poitier became the first black to win an Oscar as Best Actor (of 1963) from the Motion Picture Arts and Sciences Academy—one of Hollywood's greatest honors. The award is for his role in the film *Lilies of the Field*.

APRIL 15

Birthday of Asa Philip Randolph (1889–   )

On July 11, 1941, a call to Negro America to march on Washington for jobs and equal participation in national defense was proposed by labor leader A. Philip Randolph. The threat of the march led President Franklin Delano

A. Philip Randolph, as a young labor leader, delivers an address. NEW YORK PUBLIC LIBRARY, SCHOMBURG COLLECTION

Roosevelt to issue an executive order outlawing discriminatory hiring practices in defense jobs. Randolph also was instrumental in the creation of a fair employment practices committee.

Randolph was born in Crescent City, Florida, came to New York as a young boy, and attended the College of the City of New York. In 1925, he organized the Brotherhood of Sleeping Car Porters, and rose to become the first black vice-president of the AFL-CIO.

Most of his life has been spent actively engaged in the fight for improved working conditions and higher wages for black people. In 1964, the A. Philip Randolph Institute, under the direction of Bayard Rustin, was established as a civil rights educational and coordinating organization.

APRIL 15–17

NEWS NOTE—1960

The Student Nonviolent Coordinating Committee (SNCC) is organized at Shaw University, Raleigh, North Carolina. In 1969 the word "national" replaced "nonviolent."

Popularly called Snick, it is an organization of student groups engaged in civil rights protests. In 1964, SNCC members conducted the Mississippi Summer Project, which operated 150 Freedom Schools and promoted voter registration among black people.

SNCC volunteers have continued to build freedom organizations and to work in the black counties of Alabama, Georgia, Arkansas, and Mississippi. Their work is also done with groups in major inner cities, in such places as Harlem in New York and Watts in Los Angeles and in Detroit and Washington, D.C.

APRIL 16

NEWS NOTE—1869

Ebenezer Don Carlos Bassett becomes Minister Resident and Consul General to Haiti, making him the first black to

receive an appointment in the United States diplomatic
service.

APRIL 23

Birthday of William Shakespeare (1564–1616)

The works of William Shakespeare have been entertain-
ing people for centuries. The famous tragedy *Othello* has
been played by such outstanding black actors as Ira Al-

A statue of Ira Aldridge in the role of Othello stands in the Schomburg Collection of the New York Public Library. NEW YORK PUBLIC
LIBRARY, SCHOMBURG COLLECTION

dridge, Richard Hewlett, Paul Robeson, William Marshall, Earle Hyman, and James Earl Jones. As early as 1821, the African Company, in New York City, an all-black troupe, was presenting Shakespeare's plays.

Shakespeare died on April 23, 1616, in Stratford-on-Avon, England.

APRIL 29

Birthday of Duke Ellington (1899–   )

Duke Ellington, born Edward Kennedy Ellington, learned to play the piano at the age of seven. At seventeen, he composed his first musical composition and called it "Soda Fountain Rag." Since that time, he has composed

Duke Ellington (left) celebrates his seventieth birthday at a White House reception. President Nixon, at the piano, plays "Happy Birthday." UNITED PRESS INTERNATIONAL

over three thousand pieces of music ranging from popular songs to serious concert works. His music can be heard throughout the world.

In 1969, on Ellington's seventieth birthday, President Richard Nixon gave a gala White House reception in Ellington's honor and presented him with the Presidential Medal of Freedom, the highest medal the government can bestow on a civilian. At the reception Mr. Nixon stated: "In the royalty of American music, no man swings more or stands higher than the Duke."

Ellington got his nickname at school because of the fancy clothes he wore.

Did You Know That

The Harlem Globetrotters, an all-black basketball team, was organized in the 1927–28 basketball season? In the 1962–63 season, the Trotters played 162 games and won all of them.

The team, known for its antics, has played thousands of games on six of the world's seven continents. Today three separate troupes play simultaneously in different parts of the world.

MAY

A child who asks a question is not stupid.

MAY 1

Howard University, the largest center for higher education for black Americans, is founded in Washington, D.C., under an Act of Congress charter.

Today nearly 7,000 students—both black and white—attend Howard. One of the finest and largest collections of material on black history and culture—more than 300,000 volumes—is located in the Founders Library.

Howard is supported by congressional appropriations, private endowments, gifts, and fees.

MAY 5

Birthday of Adam Clayton Powell, Sr. (1865–1953)

Adam Clayton Powell, Sr., entered school on October 1, 1871, at the age of six. On the first day he learned the alphabet, and by the second day he knew it backward.

After finishing high school, Powell decided to become a minister. He continued his education and became pastor of the Abyssinian Baptist Church in New York City in 1908. In 1937, Reverend Powell retired from his position. He was

succeeded by his son, Adam Clayton Powell, Jr., who later became New York's first black congressman.

MAY 6

Birthday of Willie Mays (1931–   )

Up to bat comes Willie Mays. The pitcher winds up, throws. Mays swings. A home run! Willie Mays has hit more home runs than any other active big-league player. He is second only to Babe Ruth in the history of baseball.

Mays came to the New York Giants in 1950. Since that time he has won one award after another:

1951—Rookie of the Year
1954—National League's Most Valuable Player

Award—41 home runs; 110 runs batted
in; .345 batting average
1955—National League home run champion
—51 home runs
1965—Most Valuable Player Award—52
home runs; .317 batting average.

Mays earns one of the highest salaries in baseball.

He was born in Fairfield, Alabama. His father worked
in a steel mill; his mother died when he was a young boy.
At Fairfield Industrial School, he was an all-sports star,
playing football, basketball, and of course, baseball. At
seventeen, he began playing for the Birmingham Black

Willie Mays of the San Francisco Giants. COURTESY OF THE SAN
FRANCISCO GIANTS

Barons, of the Negro National League. It was on this team that he began to receive national attention.

When he came to New York, he lived in Harlem. Mays often played stickball in the streets, for there are few parks and playgrounds in Harlem.

Today Mays is the idol of millions.

MAY 6

NEWS NOTE—1969

Thirty-four-year-old Howard Lee is elected mayor of Chapel Hill, North Carolina. Lee, son of Georgia sharecroppers, is the first black mayor elected by a predominantly white North Carolina city in modern times. He holds a Master's degree in social work from the University of North Carolina.

MAY 9

Birthday of John Brown (1800–1859)

John Brown was a white man dedicated to abolishing slavery in the United States. Brown came to believe that the slaves would be freed only as a result of direct military action. On October 16, 1859, he and twenty-one other men carried out a plan to seize the federal armory at Harpers Ferry, Virginia. United States Marines stormed the armory

76

United States Marines storm the federal armory seized by abolitionist John Brown and his men at Harpers Ferry. NEW YORK PUBLIC LIBRARY, SCHOMBURG COLLECTION

and, on October 18, Brown was captured. He was hanged for treason on December 2.

A famous marching song of the Civil War commemorates him.

The chorus which is repeated after each verse goes:

Glory, glory, Hallelujah!
Glory, glory, Hallelujah!
Glory, glory, Hallelujah!
His soul goes marching on.

Four of the verses are:

John Brown's body lies a-mouldering in the grave,
John Brown's body lies a-mouldering in the grave,

John Brown's body lies a-mouldering in the grave,
But his soul goes marching on.

He's gone to be a soldier in the army of the Lord,
He's gone to be a soldier in the army of the Lord,
He's gone to be a soldier in the army of the Lord,
His soul is marching on.

John Brown died that the slave might be free,
John Brown died that the slave might be free,
John Brown died that the slave might be free,
But his soul goes marching on.

The stars of heaven are looking kindly down,
The stars of heaven are looking kindly down,
The stars of heaven are looking kindly down,
On the grave of old John Brown.

MAY 10

Birthday of Pinckney Benton Steward Pinchback (1837–1920)

P.B.S. Pinchback, the son of a Mississippi planter and a slave, was born free in Georgia. The white planter freed Pinchback's mother and her children and sent them to Ohio, where the youngsters were educated. At the age of twelve, Pinchback became cabin boy on a riverboat; before long he was promoted to steward. During the Civil War he joined the Union army and raised a company of black volunteers called the Corps d'Afrique. Later he became captain of the Louisiana Native Guards, a company of black cavalry.

After the war Pinchback entered Louisiana politics and worked to organize the Republican party. He served in the state senate, as lieutenant governor, and, for little over a month, as acting governor. On two occasions he was elected to an office for which he was never seated. First, he was elected congressman-at-large, but his Democratic opponent successfully contested the race. In the second case, he was elected to the Senate, but after a three-year fight, he was denied his seat. In 1877, Pinchback became a Democrat.

At the age of fifty he began to study law, and although he was admitted to the state bar, he never practiced. In 1890, he moved to Washington, D.C., where he remained until his death.

Composer William Grant Still. NEW YORK PUBLIC LIBRARY, SCHOMBURG COLLECTION

MAY 11

Birthday of William Grant Still (1895–   )

William Grant Still is the first known black composer of symphonic music. Among his most famous works are: *Afro-American Symphony, Africa,* and *Symphony in G Minor: Song of a New Race.*

Mr. Still was born in Woodville, Mississippi.

Former world heavyweight champion Joe Louis (right) gives advice to Canadian boxer George Chuvalo. UNITED PRESS INTERNATIONAL

MAY 13

Birthday of Joe Louis (1914–   )

Joe Louis was born Joseph Louis Barrow in a sharecropper shack near Lafayette, Alabama, but moved to Detroit as a young boy. His first professional fight took place in 1934, when he won a heavyweight bout against Jack Kracken. Louis was paid $59 for the bout, the first in a career that carried him to the world heavyweight championship.

Louis retired from boxing in 1951. He had fought in 71 bouts and had won 68 of them—54 by knockouts—earning him the nickname, The Brown Bomber.

MAY 13

NEWS NOTE—1969

Civil rights leader Charles Evers wins the Democratic primary for mayor in Fayette, Mississippi. Because Evers will be unopposed in the general election June 3, his election is assured. In spite of Fayette's small population of two thousand (including twelve hundred blacks), the victory of a black candidate in Mississippi is significant and shows the possible effects of intensive black-voter registration drives.

MAY 19

NEWS NOTE—1910

The National Urban League is formed by George Edmund Haynes, a black sociologist, to help blacks adjust to city life. The League is a voluntary community service agency of civic, professional, business, labor, and religious leaders dedicated to ending segregation and discrimination based on creed or color. Like the National Association for the Advancement of Colored People, the League has both black and white members.

In the period beginning with World War I, great numbers of black sharecroppers left the South to take advantage of better job opportunities in large Northern cities. This migration has continued until today. The National Urban League tries to provide the newcomers with educational and job opportunities.

Since 1961, Whitney M. Young, Jr., has headed the organization as executive director.

MAY 19

Birthday of Malcolm X (1925–1965)

Malcolm X, born Malcolm Little, became famous as a leader of the religious movement named the Nation of Islam, but often called the Black Muslims. The organization was formed in Detroit in 1930. Many Black Muslims take the letter X as a last name to replace the family names given by white slave owners to their slaves. The Black Muslims seek to cast off the identity given to African slaves

Slain black leader Malcolm X. UNITED PRESS INTERNATIONAL

by their white masters and to reestablish the black man's pride in his own heritage.

In 1964, Malcolm X broke away from the Black Muslims and formed the Organization of Afro-American Unity— a protest movement which advocated separation of the races. The members of his new organization sought to unify, dignify, and reshape the character of the black masses. Malcolm X himself had risen from a sordid and squalid background to become a powerful spokesman for black nationalism.

On February 21, 1965, Malcolm X was shot and killed while delivering a speech to his followers in New York City. His dedication to his people was greatly admired by many Americans.

MAY 19

Birthday of Lorraine Hansberry (1930–1965)

Lorraine Hansberry was the first black playwright to win the New York Drama Critics Circle Award. She received the award for her play *A Raisin in the Sun*, which deals with a black family preparing to move into a white neighborhood. The play opened on Broadway on March 11, 1959, and was later made into a film. Sidney Poitier starred in both productions.

Miss Hansberry was born in Chicago, Illinois, and died in New York City, on January 12, 1965, not long after the opening of her play *The Sign in Sidney Brustein's Window*.

MAY 25

Birthday of Bill "Bojangles" Robinson (1878–1949)

Bill Robinson, vaudeville dancer and star of stage and screen, was known as the King of Tap Dancers. He appeared in fourteen motion pictures, many with child-star Shirley Temple, including *Rebecca of Sunnybrook Farm* and *The Little Colonel*. In 1932, he received top billing in the first all-Negro talking movie, *Harlem Is Heaven*.

He was born in Richmond, Virginia, and died on November 25, 1949, at the age of seventy-one.

MAY 26

NEWS NOTE—1826

John B. Russwurm graduates from Bowdoin College in Maine, becoming the first black person to graduate from an American college.

MAY 29

Birthday of John Fitzgerald Kennedy (1917–1963)

Let the word go forth from this time and place, to friend and foe alike, that the torch has been passed to a new generation of Americans. . . .

—Inaugural Address, January 20, 1961

President John F. Kennedy (center) meets with, from left to right, Dr. Martin Luther King, Roy Wilkins, Dorothy Height, and A. Philip Randolph at a White House talk on greater participation of American blacks in African policies. UNITED PRESS INTERNATIONAL

No one has been barred on account of his race from fighting or dying for America—there are no "white" and "colored" signs on the foxholes and graveyards of battle. Surely, in 1963, one hundred years after emancipation, it should not be necessary for any American citizen to demonstrate in the streets for the opportunity to stop at a hotel, or to eat at a lunch counter in the very department store in which he is shopping, or enter a motion picture house, on the same terms as any other customer.

—Speech of June 19, 1963

MAY 30

Birthday of Countee Cullen (1903–1946)

Countee Cullen, one of America's leading black poets, was born Countee Porter in Baltimore, Maryland. Orphaned at an early age, he was adopted by Reverend Frederick Cullen of New York City. After attending public school

Poet Countee Cullen. NEW YORK PUBLIC LIBRARY, SCHOMBURG COLLECTION

in New York, Cullen went on to New York University and then to Harvard University, where he received his Master of Arts degree.

Color, his first book of poetry, was published in 1925, while he was still a student. His book *The Lost Zoo* is considered a children's classic. It contains "The Animals That Went Into the Ark," a funny animal poem. In it Cullen gives the animals such names as Hazel Hind, Atom Ant, L. E. Phant, Michael Monkey, and Donald Donkey.

At the time of his death, January 9, 1946, Cullen was a teacher of French at a public high school in Harlem.

Did You Know That

Frances Ellen Watkins Harper (1825–1911) was the first black woman to publish a novel?

The title of her book was *Iola LeRoy: The Shadows Lifted*. It appeared in 1892.

JUNE

African Proverb

Patience is the key of well being.

JUNE 1

NEWS NOTE—1968

California-born Henry Lewis becomes the first black musical director of an American symphony orchestra by taking leadership of the New Jersey Symphony. Lewis was formerly an associate director of the Los Angeles Philharmonic.

Conductor Henry Lewis. UNITED PRESS INTERNATIONAL

JUNE 3

Birthday of Roland Hayes (1887–)

Roland Hayes, born in Curryville, Georgia, was the first black concert artist to receive acceptance in the United

States. He has been hailed by music critics the world over and has been called "the greatest tenor ever born in America."

JUNE 3

Birthday of Charles Richard Drew (1904–1950)

Charles Drew, a doctor and scientist, was born in Washington, D.C. His discovery of a process to change blood into plasma saved thousands of lives during World War II. In 1941, when the American Red Cross set up blood donor stations to collect blood plasma for the armed forces, Drew was appointed director of the project.

Later, he became chief of the surgery department at Howard University, in Washington, D.C. Although his career ended abruptly in April, 1950, when he was killed in an automobile accident, the research that he did continues to save lives throughout the world.

Dr. Charles Drew, who saved countless lives all over the world through his discovery of a process to change blood into plasma. SCURLOCK PHOTO FROM THE AMERICAN RED CROSS

Birthday of Roy Innis (1934–   )

Roy Innis was born in St. Croix, Virgin Islands. He came to the United States at the age of twelve and lived with his family in Harlem in New York City. He attended the College of the City of New York, where he majored in chemistry.

In October, 1965, he was elected chairman of the Harlem chapter of the Congress of Racial Equality. On June 26, 1968, he replaced Floyd McKissick as executive director of the national chapter.

Roy Innis succeeded Floyd McKissick as executive director of the national chapter of the Congress of Racial Equality. UNITED PRESS INTERNATIONAL

Birthday of Gwendolyn Brooks (1917–   )

Gwendolyn Brooks was born in Topeka, Kansas, but spent most of her life in Chicago. At the age of thirteen, she wrote a poem called "Eventide," which was accepted by *American Child Magazine*. This encouraged her to continue writing.

In 1950, Gwendolyn Brooks became the first black person to win a Pulitzer Prize. She was awarded this honor for her book of poems entitled *Annie Allen*. In 1956, she published *Bronzeville Boys and Girls*, a collection of poems for children. Some other books by Miss Brooks include a novel, *Maud Martha* (1953), and three other books of poems, *The Bean Eaters* (1960), *Selected Poems* (1963), and *In the Mecca* (1969). In 1968, Gwendolyn Brooks was named Poet Laureate for the state of Illinois, succeeding the late Carl Sandburg.

Poetess Gwendolyn Brooks, the first black writer to win the Pulitzer Prize. NEW YORK PUBLIC LIBRARY, SCHOMBURG COLLECTION

JUNE 8

NEWS NOTE—1953

Supreme Court ruling bans discrimination in Washington, D.C., restaurants. Until this date, many restaurants have refused to serve black customers. The Court's decision was very important since Washington is the national capital and sets the tone for the rest of the country.

JUNE 10

NEWS NOTE—1854

At the age of twenty-four, James Augustine Healy is ordained a priest in Notre Dame Cathedral, in Paris. On June 2, 1875, he becomes the first black American Roman Catholic bishop.

JUNE 10

Birthday of Hattie McDaniel (1898–1952)

Hattie McDaniel became the first black performer to win an Oscar, the Motion Picture Academy's highest award. She won this honor for her role as supporting actress in the film *Gone With the Wind*.

She was born in Wichita, Kansas. She died on October 26, 1952.

Slain civil rights leader Medgar Evers (with sign around neck) is arrested with Roy Wilkins in Jackson, Mississippi, June 1, 1963.
UNITED PRESS INTERNATIONAL

JUNE 12

Death of Medgar Wiley Evers (1926–1963)

Medgar Evers was shot and killed in Jackson, Mississippi, during a civil rights demonstration. He had served as a field secretary for the National Association for the Advancement of Colored People in Mississippi.

Mr. Evers was posthumously awarded the Spingarn Medal in 1963.

JUNE 13

NEWS NOTE—1868

Oscar J. Dunn, an ex-slave, is formally installed as lieutenant governor of Louisiana. It is the highest elective office held by a black American up to this time.

JUNE 14

Birthday of Harriet Beecher Stowe (1811–1896)

Harriet Beecher Stowe will be remembered for her novel *Uncle Tom's Cabin*, which described the inhuman conditions under which slaves were forced to live. Several hundred thousand copies were published in the first year, and since that time millions of copies have been sold and the book has been translated into many languages. The char-

Harriet Beecher Stowe, author of *Uncle Tom's Cabin*. NEW YORK PUBLIC LIBRARY, PICTURE COLLECTION

acters Tom, Little Eva, and the brutal Simon Legree became known throughout the world.

It has been said that *Uncle Tom's Cabin* helped to start the Civil War—and win it. No other novel in the history of America has played such a part in politics.

JUNE 15

NEWS NOTE—1877

Henry O. Flipper becomes the first black student to graduate from the United States Military Academy at West Point.

Henry O. Flipper, while a cadet at West Point. NEW YORK PUBLIC LIBRARY, SCHOMBURG COLLECTION

JUNE 17

Birthday of James Weldon Johnson (1871–1938)

On December 12, 1900, James Weldon Johnson wrote the words, and his brother, James Rosamund Johnson, wrote the music to a song which they called "Lift Every Voice and Sing."

Originally written in honor of Abraham Lincoln's birthday celebration, it has since been called the Negro National Anthem.

> Lift every voice and sing
> Till earth and heaven ring,
> Ring with the harmonies of Liberty;
>
> Let our rejoicing rise
> High as the listening skies,
> Let it resound loud as the rolling sea.
>
> Sing a song full of the faith that the
> dark past has taught us,
> Sing a song full of the hope that the
> present has brought us,
> Facing the rising sun of our new day
> begun
> Let us march on till victory is won. . . .

James Weldon Johnson also has a place in history as an author, educator, and statesman. He was the first black lawyer admitted to the Florida bar. Between 1906 and 1912 he served as a United States consul in Venezuela and Nicaragua. He was a professor at Fisk University and New York University. His book *The Autobiography of an Ex-*

Brothers James Weldon (left) and James Rosamund Johnson. UNITED PRESS INTERNATIONAL (LEFT) AND NEW YORK PUBLIC LIBRARY, SCHOMBURG COLLECTION (RIGHT)

Colored Man, published in 1912, dealt with the problems of a black man in white society. Johnson will be remembered also as a founder of the National Association for the Advancement of Colored People (NAACP).

JUNE 20

Birthday of André Watts (1946–   )

Concert pianist André Watts made his first public appearance at the age of nine, when he performed at a children's concert in Philadelphia. Solo performances with the Philadelphia Orchestra followed. On January 31, 1963, Watts

100

was called upon to substitute for pianist Glenn Gould in a solo performance with the New York Philharmonic. He received a standing ovation from both the audience and the orchestra. *The New York Times* described him as possessing an "indefinable electric quality."

Watts was born in Nuremberg, Germany, the son of a black American serviceman and a Hungarian mother.

JUNE 21

Birthday of Carl B. Stokes (1927–   )

Carl Stokes rose from a life of poverty in the slums of Cleveland, Ohio, to become mayor of his city—the first black to be elected head of a major United States city.

Carl B. Stokes and his wife greet crowds of well-wishers after Stokes is sworn in as mayor of Cleveland. UNITED PRESS INTERNATIONAL

Before taking office as mayor in November, 1967, Stokes practiced law and was a member of the Ohio State Legislature.

JUNE 22

Birthday of Katherine Dunham (1910–   )

Katherine Dunham is one of the world's most famous modern dancers and choreographers. She has performed her primitive dances, adapted from tropical cultures, in the United States and Europe. Miss Dunham's studies in anthropology at the University of Chicago were useful in developing her dancing style.

JUNE 24

Birthday of Henry Ward Beecher (1813–1887)

Henry Ward Beecher was the brother of Harriet Beecher Stowe, author of *Uncle Tom's Cabin*—a famous antislavery novel.

Beecher was an American Congregationalist minister, lecturer, and abolitionist. On June 1, 1856, he held a mock auction of a black girl in his church (the Plymouth Church, Brooklyn, New York) to demonstrate the cruelty of slavery.

Mr. Beecher was one of the greatest speakers of his time.

JUNE 25

NEWS NOTE—1941

President Franklin Delano Roosevelt issues Executive Order No. 8802, which establishes the Fair Employment Practices Commission, to prohibit discrimination in defense industries or government because of race, creed, color, or national origin.

JUNE 30

Birthday of Lena Horne (1917–   )

Lena Horne was born in Brooklyn, New York. At the age of sixteen, she joined the chorus line at the Cotton Club, a famous nightclub in New York's Harlem. Later she toured as a dancer, acted on the stage, sang with big bands, and became the first black woman to sign a term contract for Hollywood motion pictures. In recent years, Miss Horne has continued to make recordings and has appeared on many television variety shows.

Singer Lena Horne. UNITED PRESS INTERNATIONAL

Black troops serving in World War I march up Fifth Avenue in New York City. BROWN BROTHERS

Did You Know That

There were 371,710 blacks in the United States armed forces during World War I?

JULY

The African race is like an India-rubber ball. The harder you bounce it to the ground, the higher it will rise.

JULY 1

Birthday of Walter White (1893–1955)

Walter White was born in Atlanta, Georgia. He was a great civil rights leader; in 1937, the National Association for the Advancement of Colored People awarded him the Spingarn Medal, for his personal investigation of forty-one lynchings and for his skill in lobbying a federal antilynching bill during President Truman's administration. Mr. White was active in forming the NAACP and served as the organization's executive secretary.

He died on March 21 in New York City.

Civil rights leader Walter White (holding papers) walks beside Mrs. Eleanor Roosevelt and President Harry Truman to the thirty-eighth annual conference in 1947 of the NAACP. UNITED PRESS INTERNATIONAL

Birthday of Thurgood Marshall (1908–   )

Thurgood Marshall studied at Lincoln University, setting out to become a dental student. With a change of mind, he entered Howard University Law School, and graduated in 1933 at the top of his class.

Marshall joined the staff of the National Association for the Advancement of Colored People as its chief legal counsel. Many of the cases that he brought to court involved racial segregation in public schools. When the case of *Brown* v. *Board of Education* was brought before the Supreme Court in 1952, it raised the question of whether segregated schools were offering inferior education to black children.

Supreme Court Justice Thurgood Marshall (rear right) with the other justices serving at the time of his appointment to the highest court in the United States. UNITED PRESS INTERNATIONAL

Two years later, the court ruled that segregated education was unequal, reversing the separate-but-equal policy established in 1896 by the decision in the *Plessy* v. *Ferguson* case.

Marshall went on to become a federal judge in the United States Court of Appeals for the Second Circuit. In 1965, he became the first black to serve as Solicitor General of the United States. Two years later, President Lyndon Johnson appointed him to the Supreme Court, making him the first black justice on the Court.

JULY 2

NEWS NOTE—1964

President Lyndon Baines Johnson signs into law a civil rights bill containing strong provisions to secure equal access in public accommodations and employment.

JULY 4

NEWS NOTE—1827

Slavery is abolished in the state of New York.

JULY 4

NEWS NOTE—1881

Tuskegee Institute, a single shack with thirty students and a faculty of one—Booker T. Washington—is opened in Tuskegee, Alabama. The next year, Washington moves this first school for the training of black teachers to a 100-acre plantation.

In 1896, George Washington Carver joined the faculty as director of agricultural research. Today Tuskegee covers nearly 5,000 acres, has more than 150 buildings, and is internationally known for agricultural research.

A laboratory at Tuskegee Institute in Alabama. POLK'S STUDIO, TUSKEGEE INSTITUTE

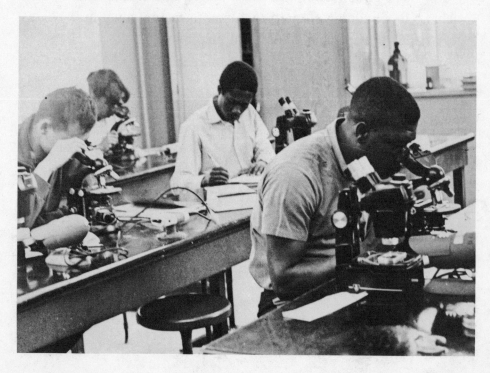

JULY 4

Birthday of Louis Armstrong (1900–   )

Louis Armstrong was born in New Orleans, Louisiana —the birthplace of jazz itself. Armstrong is known by the nickname Satchmo, and is the acknowledged king of jazz.

"The King of Jazz," Louis Armstrong. ASSOCIATED BOOKING CORP.

JULY 7

Birthday of Margaret Walker (1915–   )

Poet Margaret Walker was born in Birmingham, Alabama. She has been honored many times for her work. In 1942, she won the Yale University Younger Poets Award for her book *For My People*.

Mrs. Walker has taught at several Southern colleges. She now lives in Jackson, Mississippi.

JULY 10

NEWS NOTE—1893

Dr. Daniel Hale Williams makes medical history by performing the first successful heart operation on record. The operation is performed at Provident Hospital in Chicago.

JULY 10

Birthday of Mary McLeod Bethune (1875–1955)

If you were to rank the great women of America, Mary McLeod Bethune would have to be high on your list. The Bethune-Cookman College, in Daytona, Florida, which she helped found in 1904, grew into one of the largest institutions for the training of black teachers in the southeastern United States.

During the great depression of the 1930's, Mrs. Bethune worked with President Franklin Delano Roosevelt and Mrs. Roosevelt to help young people. Mrs. Bethune served as the director of the Negro Affairs division of the National Youth Administration. This organization helped more than half a million black students to stay in school during these difficult years.

Mary McLeod Bethune helping black servicemen during World War II. NEW YORK PUBLIC LIBRARY, SCHOMBURG COLLECTION

Mrs. Bethune died on May 18, 1955. She wrote in her last will and testament:

I leave you love; I leave you hope; I leave you the challenge of developing confidence in one another; I leave you a thirst for education; I leave you a respect for the use of power; I leave you faith; I leave you racial dignity; I leave you a desire to live harmoniously with your fellow men; I leave you a responsibility to our young people.

113

JULY 11–13

During these few days, a group of young militant black intellectuals met at Niagara Falls in Canada in an attempt to work out solutions to the many racial problems in the United States. The group's leader, W.E.B. DuBois, criticized the programs and philosophy of Booker T. Washington, who advocated forgoing equality until the black man achieved training in manual and industrial skills. DuBois wanted immediate full equality, and stated:

> We want the Constitution of our country enforced. . . . We want our children educated. . . . We are men and we want to be treated as men! We will be treated as men. And we shall win!

The movement was termed the Niagara Movement and its prime purpose was to end racial discrimination.

In later years, the group joined with white people to form the National Association for the Advancement of Colored People.

JULY 15

NEWS NOTE—1779

During the American Revolution, a slave named Pompey delivered food to British troops that had captured the fort at Stony Point on the Hudson River. As part of a plan to help the Americans, Pompey persuaded the British to let him make his deliveries after dark. On the night of July 15, after Pompey was admitted to the fort, American troops under the command of General Anthony Wayne entered and recaptured the strategic fort.

Although Pompey's role in the American victory was acknowledged, he was soon forgotten. There is no record of his birth or death.

JULY 15

Birthday of Maggie Lena Walker (1867–1934)

Born in Richmond, Virginia, Maggie Walker became the first black founder and president of a bank in the United States. The institution was the St. Luke Bank and Trust Company in Richmond.

Banker Maggie Lena Walker. THE AS-
SOCIATED PUBLISHERS, INC.

JULY 16

Birthday of Ida B. Wells Barnett (1862–1931)

Ida B. Wells Barnett was born in Holly Springs, Mississippi. Always interested in journalism, she managed to buy a half-interest in the *Free Speech*—a Memphis, Tennessee, newspaper. She built the business up until she was finally able to buy out her partner and edit the paper the way she saw fit. She wrote about the poor treatment of blacks in Memphis and urged them to go north. She also conducted an antilynching campaign during the 1890's, when over one thousand blacks were murdered or lynched and not one person was put on trial.

Moving to New York, she continued to work as a journalist, becoming an outstanding editor. Mrs. Barnett was one of the founders of the National Association for the Advancement of Colored People; she also founded the first federation of Negro Women's Clubs.

Mrs. Barnett died in 1931. Today there are many organizations named after her, as well as a large housing development in Chicago, Illinois.

JULY 17

Birthday of Diahann Carroll (1935–   )

Diahann Carroll has the distinction of being the first black actress to appear in her own television series, "Julia." The series brought the talents and beauty of Miss Carroll to the attention of millions of Americans.

Diahann Carroll was born in New York City. She began her career in show business as a model. Later she turned her attention to acting and singing, and appeared in films and on the Broadway stage.

JULY 24

Birthday of Ira Aldridge (1804?–1867)

Although Ira Aldridge was born in the United States, it was in Europe that he became known as an outstanding Shakespearean actor. During this period, slavery had prevented black Americans from utilizing their abilities. On April 10, 1833, London acclaimed his performance as Othello. He went on to perform in all the great capitals of Europe.

Aldridge died in 1867 in Poland. Today he is honored by a tablet at the New Memorial Theatre, Stratford-on-Avon, England.

Ira Aldridge as Othello. NEW YORK PUBLIC LIBRARY, SCHOMBURG COLLECTION

Psychologist Kenneth B. Clark. UNITED PRESS INTERNATIONAL

JULY 24

Birthday of Kenneth Bancroft Clark (1914–   )

Dr. Kenneth B. Clark was born in the Panama Canal Zone. He received his Bachelor of Arts degree in 1935 from Howard University, is Master of Science degree in 1936, and his Ph.D. in 1940 from Columbia University. Most of his life has been spent in the field of education, as a teacher and writer.

Dr. Clark, a specialist in the education of children, contributed the psychological research used by the National

Association for the Advancement of Colored People in its challenge to segregated education. Information he gathered showing the psychological effects of prejudice on blacks was presented to the Supreme Court before it handed down its decision in favor of integrated schooling on May 17, 1954. In 1961, he was awarded the Spingarn Medal for his outstanding achievements in educational psychology and for organizing the Northside Center for Child Development.

Dr. Clark's plan for the early education of the disadvantaged was the basis for HARYOU-ACT, a community action project, which provides a head start for young children, helps cure and treat narcotic addicts, and trains young school dropouts for jobs.

In 1966, the New York State Legislature appointed Dr. Clark to the State Board of Regents, making him the first black to serve on that body.

The Metropolitan Applied Research Center was founded by Dr. Clark to help poor blacks in large cities.

JULY 26

NEWS NOTE—1948

President Harry S Truman issues Executive Order No. 9981, establishing "equality of treatment and opportunity for all persons, without regard to race, color, or national origin" in the armed forces.

JULY 28

NEWS NOTE—1868

The Fourteenth Amendment becomes part of the United States Constitution. The Amendment provides that "all persons born or naturalized in the United States, and subject to the jurisdiction thereof, are citizens of the United States. . . ."

JULY 31

Birthday of Whitney M. Young, Jr. (1921–   )

Since 1961, Whitney M. Young, Jr., has been the executive director of the National Urban League. He was born in Lincoln Ridge, Kentucky. He received a Bachelor of Science

Whitney Young, Jr., executive director of the National Urban League.

degree at Kentucky State College, a Master of Arts degree in social work at the University of Minnesota, and did graduate work at the Massachusetts Institute of Technology. From 1954 to 1961, Mr. Young served as dean of Atlanta University's School of Social Work.

In 1968, at the national convention of the Congress of Racial Equality Mr. Young advocated a more militant policy for black people based on dignity, unity, and achievement of political power.

He now lives in New Rochelle, New York, with his wife, Margaret, an author of children's books.

Did You Know That

The Negro Ensemble Company, based in New York City, was sent to London to represent the United States in the 1969 World Theater Season? The Negro Ensemble Company is a highly praised and successful dramatic group.

AUGUST

Not to know is bad; not to wish to know is worse.

AUGUST 3

NEWS NOTE—1957

Archibald J. Carey, Jr., of Illinois, is appointed the vice-chairman of the President's Committee on Government Employment Policy, becoming the first black person to hold the post.

AUGUST 7

Birthday of Ralph Johnson Bunche (1904–   )

Dr. Ralph J. Bunche, internationally famous diplomat and United Nations mediator, was the first black American to receive the Nobel Peace Prize. He was given this award in 1950 for his many years of work for peace throughout the world, and particularly for his role in 1950 in the Arab-Israeli dispute. He has also received many honorary degrees from colleges and universities throughout the United States.

Dr. Bunche was born in Detroit, Michigan; his father was a barber from Ohio, his mother, the daughter of a school-teacher. In 1927, he graduated from the University of California in Los Angeles. The following year he received his Master's degree in government from Harvard University, and in 1934 he received his Ph.D. from Harvard.

125

AUGUST 9

NEWS NOTE—1961

James B. Parsons becomes the first black United States District judge.

AUGUST 11

Birthday of Robert Brown Elliott (1842–1884)

Robert B. Elliott, one of the most brilliant black politicians of his era, was the son of West Indian immigrants. Elliott received most of his schooling far from his native Boston. He studied in Jamaica and in England, where he graduated from Eton College.

At twenty-six, Elliott was elected to the South Carolina legislative assembly. He later served two terms in the United States Congress, where he fought for the passage of civil rights legislation.

Nineteenth-century congressman Robert B. Elliott of South Carolina served in Congress for two terms. LIBRARY OF CONGRESS

AUGUST 11

Birthday of James Rosamund Johnson (1873–1954)

The music for "Lift Every Voice and Sing," often called the Negro National Anthem, was written by J. Rosamund Johnson. His brother, James Weldon Johnson, wrote the lyrics.

James Johnson also was the arranger of many Negro spirituals, and set many of Paul Laurence Dunbar's poems to music.

AUGUST 11

Birthday of Carl T. Rowan (1925–   )

Carl T. Rowan was born in Ravenscroft, Tennessee. At the age of nineteen, during World War II, he became one of the first blacks to be commissioned as a naval officer. Rowan received a Bachelor of Arts degree from Oberlin College in Ohio, and a Master of Arts degree in journalism from the University of Minnesota. After working for the Baltimore *Afro-American*, the Minneapolis *Tribune*, and many magazines, Rowan went to work for the United States government.

He served as ambassador to Finland, director of the United States Information Agency, and as a member of the United States delegation to the United Nations.

In 1965, he became a nationally syndicated columnist and a commentator for the Westinghouse Broadcasting Company.

AUGUST 16

Death of Peter Salem (? –1816)

Peter Salem was born and died in Framingham, Massachusetts. A memorial erected in Framingham by the local chapter of the Sons of the American Revolution bears the inscription:

PETER SALEM
A soldier of the Revolution
Concord
Bunker Hill
Saratoga
Died 8/16/1816

Peter Salem (on left) at the Battle of Bunker Hill. NEW YORK PUBLIC LIBRARY, SCHOMBURG COLLECTION

AUGUST 17

Birthday of Archibald Henry Grimké (1849–1930)

Archibald Grimké, a lawyer and author of many books, including biographies and works protesting racial discrimination, was born near Charleston, South Carolina. On June 27, 1919, he was awarded the Spingarn Medal for "seventy years of distinguished service to his race and country." Grimké served the United States as a diplomat in Santo Domingo.

AUGUST 18

Birthday of Rafer Johnson (1935–   )

Rafer Johnson, the world-renowned track and field star, was born in Hillsboro, Texas. Johnson is considered one of

Olympic champion Rafer Johnson (left) on a whistle-stop tour with the late Senator Robert F. Kennedy, campaigning for the 1968 Democratic Presidential primary in California. UNITED PRESS INTERNATIONAL

the greatest athletes on record. In the 1960 Olympic Games, held in Rome, Italy, Johnson participated in the decathlon, among the world's most difficult tests of athletic ability.

The decathlon consists of ten contests: the 100-meter run, the broad jump, the shot put, the high jump, the 400-meter run, the 110-meter high hurdle, the discus throw, the pole vault, the javelin throw, and the 1,500-meter run (.9 of a mile).

Johnson scored 8,392 points in the contests, and won the decathlon gold medal and the title "the greatest all-around athlete in the world."

Johnson is currently appearing in motion pictures.

AUGUST 18

NEWS NOTE—1963

James Meredith becomes the first black graduate of the University of Mississippi.

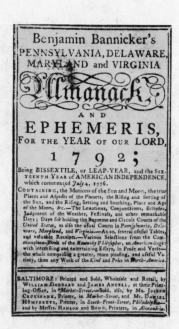

AUGUST 19

NEWS NOTE—1791

Benjamin Banneker, scientist and inventor, publishes his famous almanac.

Benjamin Banneker's *Almanack,* which first appeared in 1791, was published annually for several years. NEW YORK PUBLIC LIBRARY, SCHOMBURG COLLECTION

AUGUST 21

Birthday of Wilt Chamberlain (1936–   )

The artistry of Philadelphia-born Wilt Chamberlain is one of the most fascinating things that has ever happened to professional basketball.

Chamberlain reached the height of 6 feet 11 inches by the time he entered high school. (He is now 7 feet 1 inch!) Upon graduating he had offers of athletic scholarships from 77 major colleges and 125 smaller ones.

In the 1962–63 season with the San Francisco Warriors, he scored 3,586 points in 80 games, giving him a scoring average of 44.8 points per game. His speed and skill have well earned him all the honors he has received.

Basketball player Wilt Chamberlain (Number 13). CALIFORNIA SPORTS, INC.

Tennis champion Althea Gibson gives a young player some helpful tips. NEW YORK PUBLIC LIBRARY, SCHOMBURG COLLECTION

AUGUST 25

Birthday of Althea Gibson (1927–   )

Like many other black sports stars, Althea Gibson developed her skills on a city street. Her interest in tennis began when she learned to play paddle tennis as a youngster in New York City's Harlem. Miss Gibson twice became women's singles lawn tennis champion of the United States. In 1957–58 she reached the peak of her career, winning three important championships—the women's singles and doubles at Wimbledon, England, and the United States women's singles.

She retired undefeated and wrote her autobiography, *I Want to Be Somebody,* in 1958.

Miss Gibson was born in Silver, South Carolina.

AUGUST 28

NEWS NOTE—1963

The March on Washington

More than 200,000 Americans—people of every race and creed—march to Washington, D.C., and gather in front of the Lincoln Memorial to tell the world that they want liberty, freedom, and justice for *all*. This is one of the

Civil rights leader Bayard Rustin delivers an address at the 1963 March on Washington. UNITED PRESS INTERNATIONAL

most significant days in the history of the civil rights struggle in America.

Among the leaders of the march are Dr. Reverend Martin Luther King, Jr., A. Philip Randolph, Roy Wilkins, and Bayard Rustin.

AUGUST 29

NEWS NOTE—1968

Twenty-eight-year-old Georgia State Representative Julian Bond is nominated as a Vice-Presidential candidate at the Democratic Convention in Chicago. Bond withdraws his name from nomination because the constitutional age minimum for Vice-President is thirty-five.

AUGUST 30

Birthday of Roy Wilkins (1901–)

As executive director of the National Association for the Advancement of Colored People, Roy Wilkins is one of the best-known leaders of an organization fighting to establish the rights of black Americans.

He was born in St. Louis, Missouri, and grew up in St. Paul, Minnesota. Wilkins attended the University of Minnesota, where he studied sociology and journalism. While at the university, he started his career as a newspaperman

134

Roy Wilkins meets with President Richard Nixon at the White House.

and joined the NAACP. He served as associate secretary, later becoming editor of the organization's magazine, *The Crisis*. His work has been primarily that of developing programs to achieve equality through education, legislation, and court action.

Did You Know That

There are approximately five thousand museums in the United States?

There is a museum in Chicago, Illinois, called the Museum of African American History. Its purpose is "to develop a center of materials on the Negro to serve the research students and schools and universities of the Midwest. It gathers, preserves and displays books, relics, souvenirs, artifacts, documents, letters, pictures, art, sculpture, phonograph records, tapes and slides relating to the Negro past and present."

Is there a museum in your hometown?

SEPTEMBER

African Proverb

A drum sounds only because it is empty.

A BACK-TO-SCHOOL GAME TO PLAY

Ta Mbele

Ta Mbele, pronounced "Tom Bailey," is a game played by children in Africa. Two rows of players line up facing each other. One player, chosen to be "it," dances back and forth between the rows while the other children clap their hands in rhythm and chant "Ta Mbele." At some point, the one who is "it" stops in front of a player. At this time, both must put out one hand. The player in line tries to guess whether "it" will put out his right or left hand and hopes to put out the same hand. If he guesses correctly, he becomes "it." If not, the first "it" continues until someone makes the right guess.

SEPTEMBER 7

Birthday of Jacob Lawrence (1917–   )

The paintings of Jacob Lawrence have been purchased by the Museum of Modern Art, the Metropolitan Museum of Art, and the Whitney Museum in New York City. Lawrence, who was born in Atlantic City, New Jersey, became interested in art at the age of thirteen. He paints in a series, a group of paintings on each subject. He has done series on John Brown's activities against slavery, on the black migration from the South, and on Toussaint L'Ouverture, a leader of the slave rebellion against the French in Haiti. Lawrence's other works include paintings of Frederick Douglass and Harriet Tubman and a book about Harriet Tubman, titled *Harriet and the Promised Land*.

SEPTEMBER 9

Birthday of Richard Wright (1908–1960)

Richard Wright is the author of the novels *Uncle Tom's Children* and *Native Son* and the autobiographical *Black Boy*—books that portray black life and racism in the United States. *Native Son*, one of his most popular novels, was also produced as a play and a film. The book was translated into

Author Richard Wright (right) with musician Count Basie. UNITED PRESS INTERNATIONAL

six languages and was a Book-of-the-Month Club selection when it was published in 1940. Mr. Wright received the Spingarn Medal in 1941 for his literary achievements. When *Black Boy* was published in 1945, it too became a best seller.

Mr. Wright left the United States in 1946 to live in Paris. He died November 28, 1960.

SEPTEMBER 11

NEWS NOTE—1966

Henry W. McGee is appointed Acting Chicago Postmaster. He is the first black postmaster in Chicago's history.

SEPTEMBER 12

Birthday of Jesse Owens (1913–   )

Jesse Owens was born in Danville, Alabama, but his family moved to Cleveland, Ohio, when he was still very young. In junior and senior high school, Owens was very good in running and jumping, and several coaches encouraged him to develop his track skills. In 1932, while attending East Technical High School, in Cleveland, he gained national attention with a 9.4 clocking in the 100-meter dash. Going on to Ohio State University, he became a track star.

Olympic champion Jesse Owens. UNITED PRESS INTERNATIONAL

At the age of twenty-three, Owens was a member of the United States track team in the Olympic Games of 1936, in Berlin, German. He set three world records:

> 100-meter run—10.3 seconds
>   (Olympic and world record)
> 200-mcter run—20.7 seconds
>   (Olympic record)
> Running broad-jump—26 feet $5\frac{5}{16}$ inches
>   (New Olympic and world record which
>   was unbroken for twenty-four years)

In later years, Owens traveled throughout the world as part of a United States State Department program called Americans Abroad.

SEPTEMBER 14

Birthday of Constance Baker Motley (1921–   )

Born in New Haven, Connecticut, Constance Baker Motley became the first black woman named to a federal judgeship in the United States.

Previously Mrs. Motley had served as a lawyer for the National Association for the Advancement of Colored People and as Borough President of Manhattan in New York City.

Constance Baker Motley, the first black woman federal judge in the United States. NEW YORK PUBLIC LIBRARY, SCHOMBURG COLLECTION

SEPTEMBER 15

Birthday of Jan Ernst Matzeliger (1852–1889)

Jan Matzeliger was born in Paramaribo, Dutch Guiana. When he came to the United States in 1860, he could barely speak English.

His accomplishments as an inventor and businessman helped make Lynn, Massachusetts, the shoe capital of the world. On March 20, 1883, his invention of the lasting machine—a device that made the manufacture of shoes by machine possible—was patented.

Matzeliger died of tuberculosis on August 24, 1889, in Lynn.

SEPTEMBER 15, 1963

NEWS NOTE—1963

Cynthia Wesley, Denise McNair, Carol Robertson, and Addie Mae Collins are killed and many other children are injured when a bomb explodes in the Sixteenth Street Baptist Church in Birmingham, Alabama, during a Bible class. The bombing is the final event in a series of violent incidents that broke out when blacks sought to end segregation in Birmingham.

SEPTEMBER 20

NEWS NOTE—1830

The First National Negro Convention opens in Philadelphia.

SEPTEMBER 23

Birthday of Mary Church Terrell (1863–1954)

Mary Church Terrell's entire life was devoted to fighting for equality. She was considered a champion of the rights of women—black and white—in the United States. Even at the age of ninety, she led picket lines against segregation in Washington, D.C.

Her accomplishments in the area of civil rights are numer-

Mary Church Terrell was a fighter for women's rights and for the rights of black people. NEW YORK PUBLIC LIBRARY, SCHOMBURG COLLECTION

ous: She was the first president of the National Association of Colored Women. Today, this organization has over 100,000 members. As an early civil rights worker in the 1940's, she worked against discrimination in restaurants.

Mary Church Terrell died on July 24, 1954.

SEPTEMBER 27

Birthday of Hiram Rhoades Revels (1822–1901)

Hiram Rhoades Revels was born free in Fayetteville, North Carolina. On February 25, 1870, he took office in the United States Senate, becoming the first black man to achieve this position. For about a year he represented Mississippi, the state he adopted after the Civil War. Much of his life was devoted to church work. He was ordained a minister

Hiram Rhoades Revels, the first black United States senator, in a photograph taken by the famous Matthew Brady. LIBRARY OF CONGRESS

in the African Methodist Church and worked to organize black churches.

He died on January 16, 1901, in Holly Springs, Mississippi.

SEPTEMBER 29

NEWS NOTE—1942

During World War II, the *Booker T. Washington*, a Liberty ship, is launched at Wilmington, Delaware. The ship's captain is Hugh Nathaniel Mulzac, a black, and the crew is half white and half black. The *Booker T. Washington* is the first ship in the merchant marine to have an integrated crew and a black captain.

America's Liberty ships were used to carry supplies to soldiers in Europe.

Did You Know That

Captain Edward Joseph Dwight, Jr., was the first black astronaut in the United States space training program?

OCTOBER

African Proverb

A roaring lion kills no game.

OCTOBER*

October is the treasurer of the year,
    And all the months pay bounty to her store;
The fields and orchards still her tribute bear,
    And fill her brimming coffers more and more.
But she, with youthful lavishness,
Spends all her time in gaudy dress,
    And decks herself in garments bold
    Of scarlet, purple, red and gold. . . .

PAUL LAURENCE DUNBAR

OCTOBER 2

Birthday of Nat Turner (1800–1831)

One of the major slave revolts of the nineteenth century was led by Nat Turner, a Virginia slave preacher. In 1828, Turner felt that God had told him to lead his people out of bondage. He gathered a group of four followers, and together they organized a revolt. On Sunday, August 21, 1831, Turner, his four disciples, and two other slaves attacked and killed Turner's master, Joseph Travis, and his

* From *The Complete Poems,* New York: Dodd, Mead and Company, 1965.

The capture of Nat Turner, the leader of the best known of all slave rebellions. NEW YORK PUBLIC LIBRARY, PICTURE COLLECTION

entire family. The group then gathered more slaves. All that night and the following day, they went from one plantation to another killing whites, in a futile attempt to lead a liberation movement of Southern slaves.

The rebellion was suppressed and Turner went into hiding for two months before he was finally captured. He was caught on October 30, 1831, and was hanged in Jerusalem, Virginia, on November 11, 1831, along with the other leaders of the revolt.

Nat Turner's revolt is early evidence of the black people's determination to win freedom.

OCTOBER 3

NEWS NOTE—1968

The Great White Hope by Howard Sackler opens on Broadway with James Earl Jones in the starring role. The play, an adaptation of the life story of American boxer Jack Johnson, who was destroyed by racism, is greatly acclaimed.

James Earl Jones in *The Great White Hope*.

For his performance, Jones was presented with a Tony Award, Broadway's highest honor, as best actor of the year. The play also won a Pulitzer Prize. Jones, born in Mississippi in 1931, had been acting for fourteen years before this major success. He had appeared in such plays as *The Blacks, Othello,* and *Emperor Jones.*

OCTOBER 4

NEWS NOTE—1864

The first black daily newspaper, the *New Orleans Tribune*, begins publication in both French and English.

OCTOBER 13

Birthday of Arna Bontemps (1902–   )

If you go to the library and look up the name Bontemps, you will almost be sure to see several books written by this poet, editor, and author of numerous works for both children and adults. One of his most popular is *Golden Slippers*, a compilation of 108 poems by 29 black poets. When the book was published in 1941, it was the first of its kind for young readers.

Mr. Bontemps was born in Alexandria, Louisiana.

OCTOBER 15

NEWS NOTE—1945

Branch Rickey, president of the Brooklyn Dodgers, announces that Jackie Robinson will play baseball with the

Jackie Robinson as a Brooklyn Dodger.

Montreal Royals, the Dodger farm club. On April 10, 1947, Robinson began his major-league career with the Dodgers.

OCTOBER 15

NEWS NOTE—1965

The Supremes—Diana Ross, Mary Wilson, and Florence Ballard—sing at a sellout concert at Philharmonic Hall in Lincoln Center, New York. They have appeared frequently on national radio and television. Their first record, "Where Did Love Go?" paved the way to stardom. The Supremes went on to become one of the top popular recording groups in the United States.

OCTOBER 24

United Nations Day

The United Nations was founded on October 24, 1945. The United Nations Charter contains four objectives:

• To save succeeding generations from the scourge of war.
• To reaffirm faith in fundamental human rights.
• To establish conditions under which justice and respect for international law can be maintained.
• To promote social progress and better standards of life in larger freedom.

The six main organs of the United Nations are the General Assembly, the Economic and Social Council, the International Court of Justice, the Security Council, the Trusteeship Council, and the Secretariat.

OCTOBER 26

Birthday of Mahalia Jackson (1911–   )

Gospel music is the traditional music of the black church. And when one thinks of *great* gospel singing, the name Mahalia Jackson comes to mind, for her rich contralto voice is known throughout the world

Miss Jackson was born in New Orleans, the daughter of a Southern preacher. At the age of sixteen, she moved to

Gospel singer Mahalia Jackson gives a European concert in Berlin. UNITED PRESS INTERNATIONAL

Chicago, where she went to work as a hotel maid. In 1934, she made her first recording, but it was not until 1945 that she began to receive national attention with her recording of "Move On Up a Little Higher," which sold more than one million copies.

Mahalia Jackson appears on radio, television, and in concerts. (She will not work in nightclubs.) Miss Jackson sang at the 1963 March on Washington and at the funeral services for the Reverend Dr. Martin Luther King, Jr., in 1968.

OCTOBER 26

Birthday of Edward W. Brooke (1919–   )

On November 8, 1966, Edward W. Brooke won election to the United States Senate over former Massachusetts gov-

Massachusetts Senator Edward Brooke (in foreground) issues a public statement during the Poor People's Campaign in 1968. UNITED PRESS INTERNATIONAL

ernor Endicott Peabody, making him the first black senator in the twentieth century. Mr. Brooke was born in Washington, D.C.

OCTOBER 27

NEWS NOTE—1954

Benjamin O. Davis, Jr., is appointed first black general in the United States Air Force.

OCTOBER 31

Birthday of Ethel Waters (1900–   )

Ethel Waters is a woman of many talents. She is a singer and actress who has appeared on radio, television, in motion pictures, and on the Broadway stage. Miss Waters was born and grew up in Chester, Pennsylvania. While still a teenager, she was singing professionally on the stage. Later, she performed in vaudeville and nightclubs, until she finally became a dramatic star on Broadway. She appeared in both the stage and film versions of *Cabin in the Sky* and *The Member of the Wedding*.

In 1951, Miss Waters' autobiography, *His Eye Is on the Sparrow,* was published. For many years she has actively worked with Billy Graham, the noted Evangelist.

Did You Know That

Blacks were on the expeditions of such famous explorers as Cortes, Balboa, Pizarro, Velasquez, and de Soto?

NOVEMBER

African Proverb

Lack of knowledge is darker than night.

NOVEMBER

NEWS NOTE—1910

In November, 1910, volume I of *The Crisis: A Record of the Darker Ages* appears. Founded by W.E.B. DuBois, the magazine aims to publicize the work of the National Association for the Advancement of Colored People. It features stories, poems, and news events of concern to all people, with emphasis on items of special black interest.

NOVEMBER 5

NEWS NOTE—1968

Forty-three-year-old Shirley Chisholm, a Brooklyn, New York, Democrat is elected to the House of Representatives. Mrs. Chisholm, the first black congresswoman in the United States, defeats James Farmer, a founder and former director of the Congress for Racial Equality (CORE). One-time schoolteacher Mrs. Chisholm entered politics as a member of the New York State Assembly.

NOVEMBER 5

NEWS NOTE—1968

Cleveland Democrat Louis Stokes is elected to the United States House of Representatives. The Ohio congressman is a brother of Carl Stokes, who was elected mayor of Cleveland in 1967.

NOVEMBER 7

NEWS NOTE—1967

Carl B. Stokes is elected mayor of Cleveland, thereby becoming the first black mayor of a major American city.

NOVEMBER 8

NEWS NOTE—1966

Edward W. Brooke of Massachusetts is elected to the United States Senate, making him the third black senator in American history, the first since the days of Reconstruction.

NOVEMBER 9

Birthday of Benjamin Banneker (1731–1806)

Benjamin Banneker began publishing an almanac as early as 1791. His interests were many and varied. He was a mathematical genius, an inventor, and he served on the committee that planned the city of Washington, D.C.

Some of Banneker's writings can be found in the United States Library of Congress. He was born a free black in Ellicott, Maryland, a town near Baltimore.

NOVEMBER 16

Birthday of W. C. Handy (1873–1958)

William Christopher Handy is the name of a school in Florence, Alabama. The man it was named for was born in the town. Handy learned the rudiments of music in elementary school. At the age of eighteen, he left home, traveling from one Southern city to another, living on the few pennies he made singing and playing the cornet. Wherever he went, Handy listened to the songs, chants, and music of people. He composed his first song, "Memphis Blues," in 1912. Two years later he wrote one of his best-known compositions, "St. Louis Blues," which has been translated into Japanese, French, Chinese, German, Italian, Swedish, and Portuguese. By the 1930's, the "blues" were an important part of music in America and Handy was called the "Father of the Blues."

The late Senator Robert F. Kennedy campaigns in Oregon for the 1968 Democratic Presidential primary. UNITED PRESS INTERNATIONAL

NOVEMBER 20

Birthday of Robert Francis Kennedy (1925–1968)

Robert Francis Kennedy, senator from New York, made the battle for civil rights a major part of his platform while seeking the Democratic nomination for President of the United States in 1968. On June 5, 1968, while campaigning in Los Angeles, Kennedy was shot by an assassin. He died the following day.

Kennedy was attorney general under his brother, President John Fitzgerald Kennedy. In 1960 he helped push through and enforce legislation outlawing discrimination on trains and buses traveling between states.

Robert F. Kennedy committed himself to fighting for the dignity of all mankind.

NOVEMBER 24

Birthday of Robert Sengstacke Abbott (1870–1940)

Mr. Abbott was the editor and founder of the Chicago *Defender*, the only black daily newspaper in Chicago. He began printing the paper in 1905. Today, the *Defender* publishes approximately thirty thousand copies a day, and the Sunday edition is circulated in eight foreign countries.

Editor and publisher of the Chicago *Defender*, Robert Sengstacke Abbott, at the peak of his career. NEW YORK PUBLIC LIBRARY, SCHOMBURG COLLECTION

Death of Sojourner Truth (1797?–1883)

If you look up the word "sojourn" in a dictionary you will find that it means "to visit, to stay for a short while, to journey." The name "Sojourner Truth" was taken by a tall, gaunt woman who felt the Lord had called on her to travel around the United States speaking the truth about the black man's rights. Her real name was Isabella Baumfree. She was born a slave around the year 1797 in upstate New York.

On July 4, 1827, she became free under the New York Emancipation Act. During the Civil War, Sojourner Truth worked as a spy for the Union army. She died in Michigan.

Sojourner Truth traveled around the United States speaking out against slavery. COURTESY OF THE NEW YORK HISTORICAL SOCIETY, NEW YORK CITY

NOVEMBER 29

NEWS NOTE—1905

The Chicago *Defender*, edited and founded by Robert Sengstacke Abbott, and now one of the largest black newspapers in the United States, begins publication.

Did You Know That

Henry T. Blair was the first black American known to receive a patent for an invention? In 1834, the United States Patent Office granted him a patent for a corn harvester. Two years later, he received a patent for a cotton planter.

DECEMBER

African Proverb

Do not despise the gift because it is small.

DECEMBER 2

NEWS NOTE—1859

John Brown, abolitionist, is hanged for leading an attack on the arsenal at Harpers Ferry, Virginia.

Abolitionist John Brown. LIBRARY OF CONGRESS

DECEMBER 3

NEWS NOTE—1847

Frederick Douglass publishes *The North Star*.

Phillis Wheatley, who was brought as a slave to the United States from Africa, became a famous poet in the eighteenth century. NEW YORK PUBLIC LIBRARY, SCHOMBURG COLLECTION

DECEMBER 5

Death of Phillis Wheatley (1753–1784)

Phillis, a young girl from Senegal, Africa, was brought to the United States as a slave at about the age of eight or nine. A Boston tailor named John Wheatley bought her as a companion for his wife. The Wheatleys' daughter, Mary, taught Phillis to read, and the whole family encouraged her in her writing. She loved to compose poems and by 1773 (the same year she was freed) she had her work published under the title *Poems on Various Subjects*. While on a trip to England, Phillis read her poetry to royalty. She was freed when she returned to the United States.

During her adult life, Phillis suffered one tragedy after another. Her husband, John Peters, deserted her and their three children after five years of marriage. Two of her children died because of the poverty they had to endure.

Sickness took the life of Phillis Wheatley in the winter of 1784. Her youngest child died the same day. They were buried together.

DECEMBER 5

NEWS NOTE—1935

The National Council of Negro Women is founded in New York City by Mary McLeod Bethune. The council united a large number of different Negro women's organizations. Today, the council has well over a million members, who concentrate on education and voter registration.

DECEMBER 6

Birthday of William Stanley Braithwaite (1878–1962)

Poet William Braithwaite was born in Boston. He was awarded the Spingarn Medal, in 1918, for distinguished

Outstanding literary figure William Stanley Braithwaite was a poet, publisher, critic, and teacher. NEW YORK PUBLIC LIBRARY, SCHOMBURG COLLECTION

achievement in literature. Mr. Braithwaite reviewed books for the Boston *Transcript*, wrote several volumes of poetry, and published "Anthologies of Magazine Verse." This annual publication included the works of such famous poets as Vachel Lindsay and Carl Sandburg. Braithwaite died on June 8, 1962.

DECEMBER 8

Birthday of Sammy Davis, Jr. (1925–   )

On March 30, 1969, Sammy Davis, Jr., was awarded the 1968 Spingarn Medal, presented annually by the National Association for the Advancement of Colored People. The presentation was made by Senator Edward Brooke of Massachusetts, the award's 1967 recipient.

Sammy Davis, Jr., was born in New York City. He has been a professional entertainer since the age of four, when he began appearing with his father and close family friend, "Uncle" Will Mastin. The three were billed as the Will Mastin Trio.

In November, 1954, Davis lost an eye in an automobile accident. This tragedy, however, in no way harmed his career; in fact, he went on to even greater accomplishments. Davis has been acclaimed one of the world's greatest entertainers. He has appeared on radio, television, in motion pictures, and on the Broadway stage. He has made many records, and in 1966 his autobiography, *Yes, I Can,* became a national best seller.

Davis was also an important figure in the civil rights movements of the 1960's.

DECEMBER 10

NEWS NOTE—1948

The Universal Declaration of Human Rights is adopted and proclaimed by the General Assembly of the United Nations.

All human beings are born free and equal in dignity and rights. They are endowed with reason and conscience and should act towards one another in a spirit of brotherhood.

Article I

DECEMBER 10

NEWS NOTE—1964

The Reverend Dr. Martin Luther King, Jr., becomes the fourteenth American, the second black American, and, at age thirty-five, the youngest man to win the Nobel Peace Prize.

Accepting the prize in Oslo, Norway, he said he was doing so for "all men who love peace and brotherhood."

After receiving the Nobel Peace Prize, Dr. Martin Luther King is congratulated by Norwegian royalty. UNITED PRESS INTERNATIONAL

Dr. King gave his prize money, about $54,000, to the civil rights movement.

DECEMBER 12

Birthday of Benjamin O. Davis, Jr. (1912–   )

Benjamin O. Davis, Jr., is the son of the first black general in the United States Army. The younger Davis followed in his father's footsteps, for he too became a brigadier general—in the United States Air Force—and one of the outstanding young officers in World War II. He graduated from West Point in 1936. In 1944 he received a Distinguished

Brigadier General Benjamin O. Davis, Jr., of the United States Air Force. NEW YORK PUBLIC LIBRARY, SCHOMBURG COLLECTION

Flying Cross for leading the 332nd Pursuit Squadron against a German installation in France.

DECEMBER 12

NEWS NOTE—1870

Joseph H. Rainey, the first black man to serve in the House of Representatives, is sworn in as congressman from South Carolina. Rainey served five terms in the House.

DECEMBER 18

NEWS NOTE—1865

The Thirteenth Amendment to the United States Constitution, which abolished slavery in the United States, is ratified. It states that:

(1) Neither slavery nor involuntary servitude, except as a punishment for crime whereof the party shall have been duly convicted, shall exist within the United States, or any place subject to their jurisdiction.

(2) Congress shall have the power by appropriate legislation, to enforce the provisions of this article.

DECEMBER 19

Birthday of Carter Goodwin Woodson (1875–1950)

". . . the achievements of the Negro properly set forth will crown him as a factor in early human progress and a maker of modern civilization."

Carter G. Woodson was born in New Canton in Buckingham County, Virginia, to former slaves. His accomplishments were many. He received his Doctor of Philosophy degree from Harvard in 1912. In 1915, he founded the Association for the Study of Negro Life and History. He was director and editor of the *Journal of Negro History*, the author of many books, and the winner of the Spingarn Medal in 1926.

Historian Carter Woodson. THE ASSOCI-
ATED PUBLISHERS, INC.

It is through Dr. Woodson's efforts that Negro History
Week was established in 1926.

DECEMBER 23

Birthday of Henry Highland Garnet (1815–1882)

Henry Garnet was born a slave in New Market, Kent
County, Maryland. He was an active abolitionist before the
outbreak of the Civil War. Through his speeches, Garnet
tried to arouse his fellowmen to rise up against oppression
and cruelty.

In 1881, Garnet was appointed minister to Liberia, where
he died shortly after he arrived.

DECEMBER 25

Merry Christmas!

The Christmas holiday is celebrated throughout the world. In Ghana, an African state, the Ashanti tribe says *Aferihia Pa,* which means "Merry Christmas."

In some other countries this greeting is said in this way:
Glaedelig Jul   (DANISH)
Hauskaa Joulua   (FINNISH)
Joyeux Nöel   (FRENCH)
Fröhliche Weinachten   (GERMAN)
Kala Christougenna   (GREEK)
Buon Natale   (ITALIAN)
God Jul   (NORWEGIAN AND SWEDISH)
Feliz Natal   (PORTUGUESE)
S Rozhdyestvom Khristovym   (RUSSIAN)
Felices Pascuas   (SPANISH)

Did You Know That

Harlem, a black community in New York City, was originally settled by the Dutch in 1658? It was named Nieuw Haarlem after a heroic Dutch town in the Netherlands. Harlem is one of the most famous black communities in the world.

The End of the Chapter *

Ah, yes, the chapter ends today:
We even lay the book away;
But, oh, how sweet the memories sped
Before the final page was read! . . .

PAUL LAURENCE DUNBAR

* From *The Complete Poems,* New York: Dodd, Mead and Company, 1965.

INDEX

Abbott, Robert Sengstacke, 167, 169
Abernathy, Ralph David, 28, 49–50
African nations, receive independence, 44–46
Aldridge, Ira, 67–68, 117
Almanack (Banneker), 130
American Revolution, 114–115, 128
Anderson, Marian, 5, 33–35
A. Philip Randolph Institute, 65–66
Armstrong, Louis, 111
Association for the Study of Negro Life and History, 180
Attucks, Crispus, 42–43
Augusta Institute, 27

Banneker, Benjamin, 130, 165
Barnett, Ida B. Wells, 116
Basie, Count, 140
Bassett, Ebenezer Don Carlos, 66–67
Beecher, Henry Ward, 102
Belafonte, Harry, Jr., 41–42
Bethune, Mary McLeod, 112–114, 175
Bethune-Cookman College, 112
Birmingham, Alabama, church bombing, 144
Black Muslims (Nation of Islam), 82–83
Black soldiers,
  in World War I, 104
  in World War II, 113
Blair, Henry T., 170
Bond, Julian, 134
Bontemps, Arna, 154
Booker T. Washington, 147
Braithwaite, William Stanley, 175–176
Brooke, Edward W., III, 37, 157–158, 164, 176
Brooks, Gwendolyn, 94
Brown, Jim, 29
Brown, John, 76–78, 173
Brown v. *Board of Education,* 108
Bruce, Blanche Kelso, 41, 44

Bunche, Ralph Johnson, 31, 125

Carey, Archibald J., Jr., 125
Carroll, Diahann, 116–117
Carver, George Washington, 4–5, 110
Chamberlain, Wilt, 131
Chisholm, Shirley, 15–16, 163
Chuvalo, George, 80
Civil Rights Act (1968), 63–64
Clark, Kenneth Bancroft, 36, 118–119
Congress of Racial Equality (CORE), 6–7, 93, 121, 163
Cornish, Samuel E., 51
Cuffe, Paul, 12–13
Cullen, Countee (Countee Porter), 86–87

Davis, Benjamin O., Jr., 158, 178
Davis, Benjamin O., Sr., 178
Davis, Sammy, Jr., 37, 176–177
Defender, 167, 169
De Priest, Oscar, 46–47
Douglass, Frederick, 26, 29–30, 173
Drew, Charles Richard, 92
DuBois, W. E. B., 32, 62, 114, 163
Dunbar, Paul Laurence, 22–23, 127, 151, 184
Dunham, Katherine, 102
Dunn, Oscar J., 97
Dwight, Edward Joseph, Jr., 148

Ellington, Duke, 68–69
Elliott, Robert Brown, 126
Emancipation Proclamation, 3, 17, 25–26
"End of the Chapter" (Dunbar), 23, 184
Evers, Charles, 81
Evers, Medgar Wiley, 36, 96

Fair Employment Practices Commission, 103

185

Farmer, James, 6–8, 163
Fifteenth Amendment, to U.S. Constitution, 52
First all-Negro talking movie, 84
First black actress to appear in own television series, 116
First black African colony to become independent nation, 44
First black American to design U.S. postage stamp, 17
First black American elected to Hall of Fame, N.Y. University, 59
First black American known to receive a patent for an invention, 170
First black American to receive Nobel Peace Prize, 31, 125
First black appointed vice-chairman of President's Committee on Government Employment Policy, 125
First black astronaut in U.S. space program, 148
First black commander of U.S. warship, 16
First black concert artist to receive acceptance in U.S., 91–92
First black congressman from New York, 73–74
First black congresswoman in U.S., 15, 163
First black daily newspaper, 153
First black founder and president of U.S. bank, 115
First black general in U.S. Air Force, 158
First black general in U.S. Army, 178
First black graduate of University of Mississippi, 130
First black lawyer admitted to practice before U.S. Supreme Court, 21
First black man to serve in U.S. House of Representatives, 179
First black man to win Academy Award Oscar, 31, 64
First black mayor in Ohio, 4
First black men to join Union army, 30
First black musical director of an American symphony, 91
First black newspaper in U.S., 51

First black performer to win Oscar, 95
First black person to graduate from American college, 84
First black person to win Pulitzer Prize, 94
First black playwright to win New York Drama Critics Circle Award, 83
First black Roman Catholic bishop in U.S., 60–61, 95
First black singer to perform with Metropolitan Opera, 5
First black student to graduate from U.S. Military Academy, West Point, 98
First black to be elected mayor of major U.S. city, 101, 164
First black to receive appointment in U.S. diplomatic service, 66–67
First black to serve in Cabinet, 8
First black to serve as Solicitor General of U.S., 109
First black U.S. District judge, 126
First black U.S. senator, 33, 146–147
First black U.S. senator to serve full term, 41, 44
First black U.S. Supreme Court justice, 109
First black vice-president of AFL-CIO, 65
First black woman named to U.S. federal judgeship, 143
First black woman to publish a novel, 88
First black woman to sign Hollywood term contract, 103
First integrated ship in U.S. merchant marine, 147
First known black composer of symphonic music, 79
First known black woman lawyer in U.S., 15
First man to perform successful heart operation, 13, 112
First man to reach North Pole, 61
First men to die in American Revolution, 43
First movement to resettle black Americans in Africa, 12–13

186

First National Negro Convention, 145
First play written by black woman to appear on Broadway, 50
First U.S. postage stamp honoring a black person, 62
First World Festival of Negro Arts, 57
Fisk University, 6
Flemming, R. J., Jr., 42
Flipper, Henry O., 98
Fourteenth Amendment, to U.S. Constitution, 120
Freedom Rides (1961), 7
Freedom's Journal, 51

Garnet, Henry Highland, 181
Ghana, receives independence, 44
Gibson, Althea, 132–133
Gravely, Lieutenant Commander Samuel L., 16
Great White Hope, The, 152–153
Grimké, Archibald Henry, 129

Handy, W. C., 165
Hansberry, Lorraine, 50–51, 83
Harlem, 183
Harlem Globetrotters, 70
Harper, Frances Ellen Watkins, 88
Harris, Patricia Roberts, 16
Hayes, Roland, 91–92
Haynes, George Edmund, 81
Healy, James Augustine, 60–61, 95
Height, Dorothy, 85
Henry, Robert C., 4
Henson, Matthew, 61
Horne, Lena, 103
Howard University, 73
Hughes, Langston, 21–22, 36

Innis, Roy, 93

Jackson, Mahalia, 156–157
Johnson, Jack, 152
Johnson, James Rosamund, 99, 100, 127
Johnson, James Weldon, 99–100, 127
Johnson, John H., 14, 36
Johnson, Lyndon B., 15, 63, 109
Johnson, Rafer, 129–130
Jones, James Earl, 67–68, 152–153

Just, Ernest E., 28, 36

Kennedy, John Fitzgerald, 84–86, 166
Kennedy, Robert Francis, 129, 166–167
King, Martin Luther, Jr., 8–11, 27, 28, 49, 57, 85, 134, 157, 177–178
King, Mrs. Martin Luther, Jr., 27

Lawrence, Jacob, 37, 139-140
Lee, Howard, 76
Lewis, Henry, 91
Lincoln, Abraham, 3, 24–26, 30, 99
Louis, Joe, 80

McDaniel, Hattie, 95
McGee, Jesse, 141–142
McKissick, Floyd, 93
Malcolm X, 82–83
March on Washington (1963), 9, 10 11, 133–134, 157
Marshall, Thurgood, 108–109
Matzeliger, Jan Ernst, 52, 144
Mays, Willie, 74–76
Meredith, James, 130
Metropolitan Applied Research Center, 119
Mississippi Summer Project (1964), 66
Mitchell, Clarence M., Jr., 37
Morehouse College, 27
Motley, Constance Baker, 14, 143
Mulzac, Hugh Nathaniel, 147
Museum of African American History, 136

National Association for the Advancement of Colored People (NAACP), 28, 34, 36–37, 81, 96, 100, 107, 108, 114, 116, 118–119, 134–135, 143, 163, 176
National Association of Colored Women, 146
National Council of Negro Women, 175
National Urban League, 81–82, 120
Negro Ensemble Company, 122
Negro History Week, 26, 181
Negro Women's Clubs, 116
New Orleans Tribune, 153
Niagara Movement, 114

Nixon, Richard, 68–69, 135
Nkrumah, Kwame, 44
Nobel Peace Prize, 10, 31, 125, 177–178
"October" (Dunbar), 23, 151
Olden, Georg, 17
Olympic Games
   (1936), 142
   (1960), 129–130
Organization of Afro-American Unity, 83

Parsons, James B., 126
Pinchback, Pinckney Benton Steward, 78–79
Plessy v. *Ferguson,* 109
Poitier, Sidney, 31, 50, 64, 83
Pompey, 114–115
Poor People's Campaign (1968), 49, 50, 157
Powell, Adam Clayton, Jr., 73–74
Powell, Adam Clayton, Sr., 73–74
Price, Leontyne, 23–24, 36

Rainey, Joseph H., 179
Raisin in the Sun, A, 50–51, 83
Randolph, A. Philip, 64–66, 85, 134
Ray, Charlotte E., 15
Revels, Hiram Rhoades, 33, 146–147
Rillieux, Norbert, 51–52
Robeson, Paul, 62–63, 67–68
Robinson, Bill "Bojangles," 84
Robinson, Jackie, 154–155
Rock, John H., 21
Roosevelt, Franklin Delano, 64–65, 103, 112
Roosevelt, Mrs. Franklin Delano, 34, 107, 112
Rowan, Carl T., 127
Russwurm, John B., 51, 84
Rustin, Bayard, 65–66, 133, 134

Sackler, Howard, 152
Salem, Peter, 128
Shakespeare, William, 67–68
Slavery, abolished in New York State, 109

Sleet, Moneta, Jr., 27
Smalls, Robert, 58–59
Southern Christian Leadership Conference (SCLC), 28, 49, 50
Spingarn, Joel Elias, 36
Spingarn Medal, 28, 34, 36–37, 96, 107, 119, 129, 141, 175–176, 180
Still, William Glant, 79
Stokes, Carl B., 101–102, 164
Stokes, Louis, 164
Stowe, Harriet Beecher, 97–98, 102
Student Nonviolent (National) Coordinating Committee (SNCC), 66
Supremes, The, 155

Ta Mbele (game), 139
Terrell, Mary Church, 145–146
Thirteenth Amendment, to U.S. Constitution, 180
Truman, Harry, 107, 119
Truth, Sojourner, 168
Tubman, Harriet, 47–48
Turner, Nat, 151–152
Tuskegee Institute, 4, 5, 59–60, 62, 110

Uncle Tom's Cabin, 97–98, 102
United Nations, 44, 155–156, 177
Universal Declaration of Human Rights, 177

Walker, Maggie Lena, 115
Walker, Margaret, 111–112
Washington, Booker T., 59–60, 110, 114
   postage stamp of, 62
Waters, Ethel, 158
Watts, André, 100–101
Weaver, Robert C., 8, 36
Wheatley, Phillis, 174–175
White, Walter, 107
Wilkins, Roy, 36, 85, 96, 134–135
Williams, Daniel Hale, 13, 112
Woodson, Carter G., 26, 180–181
World Festival of Negro Arts, 57
Wright, Richard, 140–141

Young, Whitney M., Jr., 82, 120–121

188